T0012774

the
shelter
and the
fence

When 982 Holocaust Refugees
Found Safe Haven in America

Norman H. Finkelstein

CHICAGO
REVIEW
PRESS

Copyright © 2021 by Norman H. Finkelstein
All rights reserved
Published by Chicago Review Press Incorporated
814 North Franklin Street
Chicago, Illinois 60610
ISBN 978-1-64160-383-6

Library of Congress Cataloging-in-Publication Data
Library of Congress Control Number: 2021933622

Interior design: Sarah Olson

Printed in the United States of America
5 4 3 2

For Rosalind

contents

〰️

〰️

— 1 —

the arrival

"I cannot tell you how much we owe the United States for giving us this home."
—Chaim Fuchs

At 7:30 AM on August 5, 2019, the church bells of Oswego, New York, rang out in unison. They marked the arrival at that exact time, seventy-five years earlier in 1944, of the first of two special trains to Fort Ontario. On board were 982 men, women, and children: refugees from Nazi terror in Europe, where World War II was still raging. Their 13-day journey began on July 20, when they boarded a US Army transport ship, the USAT *Henry Gibbins*, in the harbor of Naples, Italy. With German submarines and planes on the prowl in the Atlantic, the ship was part of a convoy

The USAT *Henry Gibbins* was used to transport wounded American soldiers as well as the 982 refugees. It had special safety features, including an elaborate fire-detecting apparatus and a unique sprinkler system in case of a shipboard fire.

of cargo and transport ships guarded by US Navy warships. It was not an easy voyage: there was constant fear of enemy attack, and along with the refugees, the ship's decks were crowded with over 1,000 wounded American soldiers.

The refugees represented 18 different nationalities, with 100 of them having survived Nazi concentration camps and 231 still under the age of 21. The oldest was over 80 years of age; the youngest was a three-day-old baby named Harry Maurer. His parents were Austrian, and he was born on a US Army transport truck on the way to the ship with the help of a British doctor. For the rest of his life he was affectionately known as "International Harry." Of the 982 refugees, 874 were Jewish.

The rest were of differing Christian denominations. What they all had in common was a will to live.

The harrowing sea journey ended on the evening of August 3, when the *Henry Gibbins* sailed into New York Harbor and passed the Statue of Liberty. The refugees' welcome to America was not warm and personal but instead strictly governed by army regulations. The next morning, the refugees were taken off the ship,

Refugees being checked in at the Fort Ontario Emergency Refugee Shelter by representatives of the War Relocation Authority and the US Army.

lined up for delousing with the insecticide DDT, which
was sprayed on each of them by soldiers. Once their
threadbare clothes were also disinfected, they were
interviewed by American intelligence agents. Each
refugee wore a hastily obtained cardboard identification tag: instead of a name, there was an identifying
number. Further depersonalizing the arrivals, the tag
carried the label U.S. ARMY CASUAL BAGGAGE.
Soldiers and Red Cross volunteers who helped the
refugees off the ship were appalled by what they saw.
The arrivals "looked haggard, unshaven and generally
unkempt. . . . Their clothing was frayed and soiled. The
most noticeable lack was that of shoes. A large number of the children were barefoot." Most were thin and
frail. All were near exhaustion after their long ordeal.
A crowd of relatives and friends, who learned about
their arrival in the newspapers, was there to greet
them. Because of the tight security they could only
catch a glimpse from afar as police held them back.
One of the volunteers observed, "Some of the families here are decimated. They lost mother, father, six,
seven, eight and nine brothers, in-laws, nieces—all of
them were deported . . . and murdered in gas cham-
bers. This group has suffered more than any I know
of." The August 21 issue of *Life* magazine featured an
article about their arrival at Fort Ontario, including

Refugee going through customs inspection. The card around her neck was her only identification.

numerous photographs of the refugees and their heroic stories of survival.

Conditions improved as the refugees boarded ferries that took them across the Hudson River to Hoboken, New Jersey. The ferries were stocked with drinks and candy bars, and an army band played in the background. Some of the refugees were frightened at first when they saw the Delaware, Lackawanna & Western Railroad trains that would take them to Fort Ontario. Trains in Europe were often used to transport people to concentration camps. They soon realized that these trains were different. They would sit as passengers in the comfortable coach cars, and a hospital car was attached to carry the sick.

Their arrival at Fort Ontario resulted in another moment of panic. Although the morning was bright and sunny and the view of a shimmering blue Lake Ontario comforting, the sight of a barbed wire–topped fence encircling the shelter, guard watchtowers, and armed soldiers reminded them again of the life they had left behind. The fear quickly disappeared as the refugees were welcomed with cookies and ice cream. One woman recalled, "We had all this food, so we knew it wasn't a concentration camp."

While the adult refugees were being interviewed and fingerprinted, children felt free to explore the fort and approach the fence, where local Oswego residents gathered to watch the arrival. Local children and refugee children who couldn't speak each other's languages soon found a way to communicate. One local little girl, Susan Saunders, passed her doll through the fence as a gift to a refugee girl. When the refugee children spotted Geraldine Rossiter arriving at the fence on her bicycle,

Their first look at the heavily guarded Fort Ontario caused concern. But the sight of food and drink made the refugees feel welcome.

they used their hands to indicate they too would like to ride. Without hesitation, she, with the help of onlookers, passed the bike over the barbed wire fence. For the refugee children, this was the first sign that they were about to enjoy the childhood that had been missing from their young lives.

The refugees were delighted with the reception they received upon arrival.

Geraldine, knowing of an opening in the fence near the lake, found a way to sneak often into the shelter to be with her new friends. She later recalled, "It was fascinating, it was depressing, to think that people had to come over like cattle. That's the only way I could think of it. But . . . at least, they are not in a concentration camp, they are free." The refugees soon noticed that,

Efraim Deutscher

Efraim Deutscher lived in Vienna, Austria, where he was a cheese manufacturer. In 1938, after the Nazis provoked a night of violence against Jews known as Kristallnacht, the Jewish husband and father was arrested and sent to the Dachau concentration camp. Though he was shortly released, he saw no future in Austria and sent his two youngest children to the United States in 1939. Shortly thereafter he was arrested again, and this time he was sent to the Buchenwald concentration camp. Released four months later, he weighed only 90 pounds. After Efraim recuperated, he and his wife made their way to Italy, where they were interned in the Ferramonti refugee camp until 1944, when they were selected to come to Oswego.

without any fanfare, the armed soldiers disappeared. The fort was now run by civilians of the War Relocation Authority.

The arrivals received first views of their new "temporary" home. Wooden army barracks had been cleaned and divided up into apartments. For the refugees, who had not eaten properly in years, the abundance of food laid before them for breakfast was too much. Fearing food would run out as it had in European camps, they

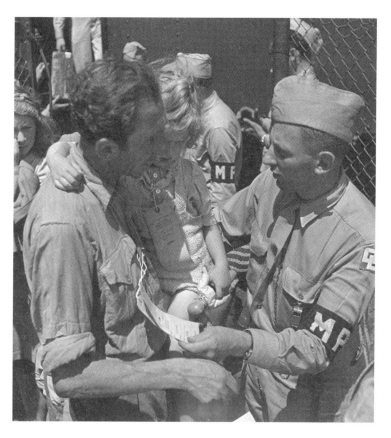

Military police at Fort Ontario checking the identification tags of a refugee father and daughter.

began hoarding whatever they could carry away, and riots nearly broke out.

"It is hard to imagine our fellow human beings awe-struck at the sight of food," a witness recalled, "but the first breakfast (corn flakes and fresh milk, eggs, fruit, toast, jam and coffee) was almost more than they could

Before settling into their new homes at the fort, the newcomers were questioned and registered.

believe possible. One little girl refused to eat an egg, because she had never seen one in her life." One woman remembered, "My first breakfast consisted of seven eggs. I ate all the bananas that I could find." Many got sick from the richness of the food.

For the next month, Fort Ontario was quarantined. Refugees could not leave, and no visitors were allowed. This was to ensure that the area was disease free and the refugees had time to adjust to their new lives and to the new food, and to realize they were safe and need not fear going hungry.

Who were these refugees?

How did they reach this point in their lives?

And what did the future hold for them?

— 2 —

marked by war

///

"They lived by their wits."
—Dr. Ruth Gruber

///

Even before coming to power in Germany in 1933, Adolf Hitler and his Nazi Party made no secret about their hatred of Jews. Looking to place blame for Germany's high unemployment and worsening economic condition after their defeat in World War I, the Nazis turned to an old hatred. Discrimination and violence against the Jewish people escalated throughout the 1930s as their rights were increasingly curtailed. Under the slogan "The Jews Are Our Misfortune," the Nazis instituted a series of programs designed to end what they called "the Jewish Problem." They began with humiliations and expulsions. Jews lost their

Signs like this appeared throughout Germany. "Whoever wears this symbol is an enemy of our people."

citizenship and could not practice their professions or trades. Jewish children could no longer attend public schools. By mid-1941, all Jews were forced to wear an identifying yellow star in public.

On the evening of November 9 into November 10, 1938, organized violence against Jews broke out throughout Nazi Germany in what came to be known as Kristallnacht, or the Night of Broken Glass. Streets of Nazi-controlled cities were littered with shards of glass from the smashed windows of Jewish-owned shops. The next day, American newspapers widely reported the beatings of Jews, burning of synagogues, and imprisonment of innocent people. It was clear: the lives of all Jews living in Nazi Germany were in peril. Discrimination and violence were only the beginning; roundups, ghettos, and concentration camps would follow.

There were few escape routes. Between 1933 and the outbreak of World War II in 1939, thousands of Jews fled from Germany and the surrounding area to Palestine, until the British government, then in control of the region, stopped Jewish immigration. Others moved to neighboring European countries, not knowing that

Jews throughout Nazi-occupied Europe were forced to wear yellow stars to both publicly identify and humiliate them. Here three Jewish cousins are shown wearing yellow stars.

their new homes would soon be overrun by invading German armies.

Meanwhile, strict laws drastically limited immigration to the United States. Years earlier, a growing

On the night of November 9–10, Nazis throughout Germany and Austria attacked Jewish institutions and businesses. It became known as Kristallnacht, or the Night of Broken Glass.

resentment of immigrants in the US led to passage of the Immigration Act of 1924, establishing a biased and restrictive quota system. "It has become necessary that the United States cease to become an asylum," said the

Adolf Hitler arrived in Paris on June 23, 1940, to celebrate Germany's occupation of France early in World War II. The arrival of German troops in conquered countries led to panic among Jewish residents.

law's author, Congressman Albert Johnson. The act limited the number of new immigrants yearly from a given country to 2 percent of the population from that country who already lived in the United States in 1890. That year was purposely selected, because an influx of Jews, Italians, Greeks, and other groups began shortly thereafter. The new regulations made it almost impossible for those groups to obtain an American visa stamped into their passports, which would grant the holder official permission to enter the country.

The strict immigration laws did not stop desperate people from trying to reach the United States. The process was maddening. First, one had to apply at the local American embassy or consulate to be placed on a waiting list to be interviewed. In 1938 Germany, the wait was over two years. Meanwhile, there were documents to gather in Germany: birth certificates, police clearances, and tax forms. Under Nazi rule, this was not an easy task. Jacob Kahn recalled, "I wrote, telephoned, telegraphed incessantly to all sort of committees, authorities, and agencies in order to get the documents."

At the same time, a sponsor—an American citizen—had to provide a written guarantee that the refugee would not become a financial burden on the United States. The sponsor had to submit bank statements, copies of tax returns, and other documentation. In a time before the internet and easy international telephoning, making connections and obtaining documents was difficult and time-consuming. If that guarantee came through, the next step was buying a ship ticket for a specific date. If there was travel involved through other countries to reach the ship, visas were also needed from those countries. All these requirements had to fit within a specific period, since some of the documents contained time limits. If even one of them expired, the whole process had to start again. Finally, if all the steps were successful, the time arrived for an interview at the American consulate to determine if the person met all the requirements and would not pose a danger to the United States.

Even then, applicants faced an unseen obstacle. In 1940, Assistant Secretary of State Breckinridge Long issued a secret memo ordering American embassies and consulates in Europe "to put every obstacle in the way and to require additional evidence and to resort to various administrative devices which would postpone and postpone and postpone the granting of the visas." Needless to say, immigration to the United States by those fleeing Nazi oppression came to a near complete stop.

Many in the United States were opposed to increasing quota numbers that would allow more immigrants into the country. One fear was that if refugees were allowed into the United States, German spies would be among them. Warnings about the possible danger appeared in important national magazines, and even President Franklin Delano Roosevelt was quoted as saying that refugees could pose a threat. At the same time that 94 percent of Americans disapproved of the Nazi attacks on Jews in Germany, 72 percent said "No" when asked if they approved of allowing a large number of German Jews to live in the United States.

Anti-Jewish feelings in America had been at a fever pitch just prior to the outbreak of World War II. Prejudice against Jews in the United States in the 1930s took many forms. Dozens of anti-Jewish organizations were founded in the US between 1933 and 1941. Father Charles Coughlin, who established the National Union for Social Justice, attracted millions of listeners to his very popular radio program, which continually broadcast anti-Jewish opinions and accused all Jews of being communists.

The German American Bund, founded in 1936 by people of German ancestry, publicly supported the Nazi agenda. The organization operated youth and training camps and had a membership across the country in the tens of thousands. On February 20, 1939, the Bund held a rally at New York City's Madison Square

Before the United States entered World War II in 1941, sympathizers in the country freely exhibited their support for the Nazi cause. Here the German American Bund parades on East 86th Street in New York City.

Garden that attracted more than 20,000 people, some dressed in Nazi-type uniforms. It featured a huge portrait of George Washington with a large swastika, the symbol of the Nazi Party, on each side. It was the era of a popular "America First" isolationist movement, which wanted to keep America out of any European conflict. One of its leaders was the hero aviator Charles A. Lindbergh, who accused American Jews of leading the country into war.

In January 1939, two members of Congress introduced the Wagner-Rogers Bill to allow 20,000 German Jewish children to enter the United States. That year, a public opinion poll asked Americans if they supported the idea of bringing Jewish refugee children from Germany into this country. Only 26 percent favored the idea; 67 percent opposed it. One opposing congressman stated, "Charity ought to begin at home. We ought to look after our own unfortunates whether they are orphans or whether they are just plain men and women of America, unemployed, before we attempt to take care of the refugee children of the world." The Wagner-Rogers Bill never passed. Just a year later, Congress did not oppose the arrival of thousands of British children seeking safety.

———

World War II began with German troops invading Poland on September 1, 1939. Other countries were soon attacked and came under Nazi rule. Those who sought refuge in neighboring European countries would soon

German troops parade through Warsaw, Poland. From the moment Germany launched its invasion of Poland, a major policy was the extermination of all Jews.

face capture or death when the Nazis invaded them, too.

The rush was on to find an escape route to safety. "In the desperate struggle for survival they lived by their wits, hid out, traveled on false passports, were interned, watched close family members dragged off to deportation and death, managed their own escape, sometimes miraculously, from camps, across frontiers, even from the windows of moving railroad cars."

On December 7, 1941, after the Nazis' Japanese allies attacked the US fleet at Pearl Harbor, the United States entered the war against Germany and Japan on the side of the Allies, which included Britain, France, the Soviet Union, and China.

Dr. Ruth Gruber was an assistant to Harold Ickes, the secretary of the interiorand head of the agency in charge of the War Relocation Authority. An accomplished journalist before the war, Gruber studied in

In response to the deportation of Jews from the Warsaw ghetto to the Treblinka concentration camp, Jewish civilians led an armed revolt during April and May 1943. When the revolt ended, survivors were rounded up by the Nazis.

What Happened to Czechoslovakia and Yugoslavia?

Today, Czechoslovakia is separated into the Czech Republic and Slovakia. Yugoslavia is split into the independent republics of Bosnia and Herzegovina, Croatia, Kosovo, Montenegro, North Macedonia, Serbia, and Slovenia.

Germany and witnessed the rise of Hitler to power. She flew to Italy to accompany the refugees aboard the *Henry Gibbins* and described their experience. "These thousand people came from 18 countries: some have been refugees since 1939, some since 1933 when Hitler took power. The path of their emigration and escape was the path of Hitler's march across Europe. He came to Germany. They fled to Austria. He came to Austria. The Germans and Austrians fled to Czechoslovakia. He came to Czechoslovakia. They fled to Poland. He came to Poland. They fled through the Balkans to Yugoslavia and from there they fled to Italy."

Nazi leaders stand at attention. Adolf Hitler is in the center row (fourth from right).

Other European Jews were not so fortunate. By the time World War II ended, 6 million would be dead. They were killed in concentration camps and by gunfire executions organized by advancing German soldiers. Their deaths and the destruction of ancient Jewish communities throughout Europe were a result of Hitler's "Final Solution" to erase an entire people. A

Entrance to the Auschwitz concentration camp. The gate bears the motto ARBEIT MACHT FREI, or "Work Makes One Free." Hundreds of thousands of Jewish men, women, and children were killed here.

Prisoners arrived at Auschwitz in crowded cattle cars, then waited to be sorted for imprisonment or death.

person's ability to escape arrest and roundup depended on not being at the wrong place at the wrong time. In many cases, it was simply a matter of luck whether an individual lived or died.

The thousands of Jewish refugees seeking safety in Italy faced many problems. One was geography. The

Simon Krauthamer

Simon Krauthamer was born in Hanover, Germany, in 1932. After the Nazis came to power, his family moved to Paris in 1935. When Paris fell to the Nazis, he and his brother were sent to live with a French family in the countryside. The family reunited later in a French town that was part of the zone occupied by Germany's Italian allies. Then, when the Germans took over the Italian zone, the family escaped by trekking over the Alps mountains into Italy. Surprised to find German forces were already there, Simon and his brother hid in a Catholic school while his mother and sister were hidden by nuns in a Catholic convent. In 1944, they reunited and registered to go to Oswego.

Students at the San Leone Magno Fratelli Maristi Catholic boarding school in Rome. In the top row at the far right is Simon Krauthamer, a Jewish child who was being hidden at the school. He arrived at Fort Ontario in 1944.

closest route to Italy from other parts of Europe went over the Alps. With little choice, groups of Jews of all ages began the difficult climb over towering icy mountains. Among them was Icek Wajc, who began the three-day journey on September 8, 1943, one of 1,000 Jews fleeing France. "We left everything behind. . . . People of 80 had to climb the Alps, 3000 meters high . . .

if they were to tell this in America they would say it is a fantasy. Famous mountain climbers can't make it. These people did it through fear." A girl remembered, "I had city clothes on. We had no blankets, no food, no provisions. Not any equipment to get over these Alps." Exhausted after their ordeals, groups found refuge in several small Italian villages on the other side.

In a dangerous escape over the Alps, Jewish refugees fled to Italy from the Italian-occupied zone in France.

The Flatau Family

Ernst Flatau and his family had left the Ferramonti internment camp and made their way to Rome. There, fearing discovery as Jews, they changed their family name to Ferrucci and lived as Catholics. One of Ernst's sons, Fred, even became a church altar boy and attended Mass. Only when the US Fifth Army liberated Rome in June 1944, did the Flataus feel safe again to reveal their real identities. They were among those selected to sail on the *Henry Gibbins*.

Twins Fred and Rolf Flatau were 13 years old when they arrived at Fort Ontario. When the shelter closed, the family moved to New York City. Both boys continued their education: Rolf became a business executive and Fred a successful physician.

With Jewish families often separated as they fled from the Nazis, children, such as these in Lyon, France, were cared for by charitable and religious organizations.

Each of the 982 refugees who arrived in Oswego came with a unique story of survival and luck, which ultimately brought them to Italy. As early as 1936, Italy's dictator, Benito Mussolini, allied himself with Germany's Adolf Hitler, but did not enter World War II until 1940. When the Italian Army captured land in France and Yugoslavia across the Italian border, it provided an escape destination for Jews and others fleeing Nazi occupation. Despite the alliance with Germany, Italians did not go out of their way to attack Jews. The Italians refused to deport Jews from their territory to

Heinz Brecher

Heinz Brecher was born in Graz, Austria, in 1932. When the Germans marched into Austria in 1938, he was sent to live with relatives in Zagreb, Yugoslavia. In 1941, when the Germans arrived there, Heinz went to the city of Split to live with family friends. In 1944, he and his new family fled by ship across the Adriatic Sea to Italy, where they were placed in displaced persons camp in Bari. His parents were killed in a Nazi concentration camp, but he was one of the 982 refugees to arrive safely in Oswego.

death in German concentration camps like Auschwitz. In fact, Joseph Goebbels, the Nazi propaganda minister, angrily complained, "The Italians are extremely lax in their treatment of Jews."

For those in Italian-controlled Yugoslavia across the Adriatic Sea, escape to Italy was by sea, with the help of anti-German fighters. Most were there without official documents and unable to find legal work. They hid in the shadows, trying not to call attention to themselves.

Italians had mixed views about their participation in the war on the side of the Nazis. In September 1943, as American and Allied troops invaded Southern Italy, Mussolini was overthrown, and on October 13, the new government declared war on Germany. For Jews who had sought safety in Italian-controlled France, Italy became their immediate destination. The Germans

The escape route over the Alps from France to Italy was difficult, but it was the only way for many to escape capture by the Nazis.

reacted by moving their troops into territories formerly held by the Italians and into Italy itself. They took control of Central and Northern Italy, including the capital, Rome. Many Jews who had survived there under Italian rule now fell into German hands. Nearly half of the Jews in the city were arrested and sent to their deaths in concentration camps in Poland. The rest went into hiding or depended on their wits for survival. Some changed their names and bought false passports to avoid detection. Others retreated to the mountains or found safety in Catholic institutions. For many, it was constant running to stay one step ahead of German soldiers.

Dr. Alexander Grin, another of the Oswego refugees, recalled, "In Rome it was terrible. In the streets, the Germans and the Fascists caught us like beasts. They blocked certain streets, caught all of us and sent us to camps or work battalions on the front. It was always an accident that I escaped the Germans. I was not on the streets when they came, or I hid in a doorway. The Italian police in Rome was very good for us; 90 percent of the people in Rome sabotaged the orders of the Germans."

Other European Jews had found sanctuary in Italian internment camps, which Mussolini's government hastily began to build in 1940 to handle the surge of refugees.

While life was difficult in the Ferramonti internment camp, there were moments of happiness too. Here children in costume are about to present a play about Snow White.

Unlike in German concentration camps, prisoners in the Italian camps were not tortured or executed—but life there was still not easy. Walter Greenberg's family, like others of the Fort Ontario refugees, found themselves in the largest camp at Ferramonti di Tarsia in Southern Italy. It was located in a marshy district and consisted of 92 barracks equipped with kitchens, latrines, and shared washbasins. Prisoners were given wooden planks on which to put thin mattresses. An Italian Jewish relief agency supported the refugees with food and books. They established a soup kitchen and a school for the children. Despite the harsh conditions, life inside was bearable, with concerts, a library, medical care, and a feeling of safety. "I must say," Greenberg later recalled, "that the Italian people were very kind as a whole . . . not that people didn't die there, not that

Life in Italian internment camps was far from comfortable. Yet, in spite of the difficulties, inmates tried to carry on close to normal activities. Here a group of children sits around a table at the Ferramonti camp.

there wasn't suffering, but there wasn't a mass program of extermination."

As the war continued, the situation of the Jewish prisoners in Italian camps worsened. Hunger and malnutrition increased as supplies of food, medicine, and clothing dwindled. To keep Germans who were retreating from Southern Italy from entering and attacking Jewish residents, camp officials raised a yellow flag at the entrance, the universal warning of a typhoid epidemic. The Germans did not enter.

On September 4, 1943, the prisoners at Ferramonti were liberated by British soldiers. However, rather than scatter, most voluntarily chose to stay in the camp. It

A group of Nazi officers prepare to conduct a search during the roundup of Jews in the city of Bydgoszcz, Poland.

Walter Greenberg

Walter Greenberg was born in Fiume, Italy, in 1933. His father was Austrian and his mother from Yugoslavia. In 1940, his father was arrested by the Italians, because he was a foreign national. Once released, he took the family to Benghazi, Libya, then occupied by Italy, where they hoped to take a ship to Palestine. But their ship never arrived, and the Greenbergs were sent back to Italy and placed in the Ferramonti refugee camp. They remained there until they escaped and went to live in a small town. But when the area fell under German control, the family then fled into the mountains. When Rome was liberated by the Allies in June 1944, they made their way there, where they heard about the American haven in Oswego.

was safer to remain there than outside, since the Allied military provided security, food, and medical care.

By the time the United States entered World War II in December 1941, news reports already hinted at terrible things happening to the Jews of Europe. But it was not until 1942 that verified details emerged of the mass killings and torture happening in German concentration camps. With war raging across the world, the American Jewish community was uncertain about how to respond. Jews wanted to be viewed as loyal Americans who supported the national war effort. They did not want to appear overly critical about the lack of world action on behalf of Europe's Jews while millions of young Americans, Jewish and non-Jewish, were heading overseas to fight.

Rabbi Stephen S. Wise, president of the American Jewish Congress, a leader of the American Jewish community and friend of President Roosevelt, believed in using private diplomacy. In a 1942 meeting in the White House, Wise told the president, "We appeal to you . . . to do all in your power to make an effort to stop" the killings. The president responded, "We shall do all in our power to be of service to your people in this tragic moment." Unfortunately, those words had no impact on millions facing certain death in Europe.

Other American Jews had little faith in the quiet diplomacy favored by Rabbi Wise. Led by Peter Bergson, a small group of activists including writers, actors, artists, and journalists staged plays, pageants, and rallies across America to openly publicize the plight of

European Jews. They placed full-page advertisements in American newspapers shaming the government's inaction to save the remaining Jews of Europe. By 1944, the intense public lobbying by Bergson and his followers began having an impact on public opinion.

Early in January 1944, a sharply worded report landed on the desk of Henry Morgenthau Jr., secretary of the treasury and a personal friend of President Roosevelt. Treasury Department staff, including Josiah DuBois and John Pehle, were upset that the State Department purposely downplayed Holocaust news and erected barriers for refugees. Their report, titled *Report to the Secretary on the Acquiescence of This Government in the Murder of the Jews*, directly accused the US government, particularly the Department of State, of purposely blocking the rescue of European Jews and others targeted by the Nazis. Morgenthau, himself Jewish, was shocked by what he read. Toning down the sharp language, he reshaped the document and handed it directly to President Roosevelt under a less accusatory title, *Report to the President*.

At the same time, public opinion in the United States regarding Jews had undergone a dramatic reversal since 1938. News of the atrocities committed by the Nazis was now common knowledge. In a Gallup poll taken in April 1944, 70 percent of Americans now favored giving

A board of directors meeting of the War Refugee Board (from left to right): Cordell Hull, secretary of state; Henry Morgenthau, secretary of the treasury; Henry L. Stimson, secretary of war; and John Pehle, executive director

"temporary protection and refuge to those people in Europe who have been persecuted by the Nazis." This gave President Roosevelt a political excuse for moving forward on aiding European refugees. The pressure on him to finally take meaningful action was too great to ignore.

On January 22, 1944, President Roosevelt issued an executive order setting up the War Refugee Board. Its purpose was "to take action for the immediate rescue from the Nazis as many as possible of the persecuted minorities of Europe, racial, religious or political, all civilian victims of enemy savagery." To head the Board, the president chose John Pehle of the Treasury Department, who had first alerted Secretary Morgenthau about government roadblocks preventing aid to European Jews. The order gave full responsibility to the board for "the rescue, transportation, maintenance and relief of the victims of enemy oppression, and the establishment of havens of temporary refuge for such victims."

In his CBS radio news program on February 21, 1944, reporter Quincy Howe spoke about the War Refugee Board. "From now on," he told listeners, "it is going to be the policy of the United States to use its power to get some millions of helpless persecuted people in Europe out of the hands of the Germans. It is to be a life-saving expedition—nothing more and nothing less. . . . It has always been the policy of the United States government and the desire of the American people to save human lives." The work of the board proceeded slowly in the beginning, as other countries lacked enthusiasm in opening shelters for refugees.

To set an example for other countries, the president wrote on June 9, 1944, "I feel it is important that the United States indicate that it is ready to share the burden of caring for refugees during the war. Accordingly, I have decided that approximately 1,000 refugees

should be immediately brought from Italy to this country, to be placed in an Emergency Refugee Shelter
to be established at Fort Ontario near Oswego, New
York, where under appropriate security restrictions
they will remain for the duration of the war." The fort,
established in 1755 on the shore of Lake Ontario, had
recently been abandoned by the US Army. It was familiar to a president who, as governor of New York, had
visited Fort Ontario on several occasions. Italy was chosen as the selection site, since the number of refugees
from liberated areas there had begun to overtax army
facilities.

It didn't hurt matters that the City of Oswego, with
a population of 20,000, welcomed new activity at the
fort after the last army trainees left in March. City residents had positive experience in the recent past dealing
with unfamiliar situations. The nearly all-white community welcomed the stationing of African American
soldiers at the fort earlier in the war. So prototypically
American was Oswego, it was selected by the army
as the subject of a documentary film shown overseas
to represent an average American city. It depicted
their open-minded attitudes by highlighting how they
turned United Nations Day into United Nations *Week*
in 1943. Local residents welcomed soldiers from other
Allied countries with a parade, a carnival, and home

hospitality. They cemented friendships by living, eating, and socializing with each other.

On June 12, President Roosevelt informed Congress of his plan. To avoid a conflict with existing strict immigration laws, the president made it clear that the refugees "will be brought into this country outside the regular immigration procedure . . . [and] at the end of the war they will be returned to their homelands." In effect, the refugees would be the personal guests of the

United Nations soldiers marching in the Flag Day parade during United Nations Week in Oswego, New York, in 1943.

president, without the right to immigrate to the United States. In a letter to the War Refugee Board overseas representative in charge of selecting refugees, Executive Director John Pehle emphasized, "Care should be used not to oversell the project. Refugees should be instructed only that they will be offered safety, security, and shelter for the duration."

In selecting candidates for the Fort Ontario Emergency Refugee Shelter, guidelines were followed to create a miniature self-sufficient community. With time of the essence, it was hoped that the selected group would include family units, at least one doctor and one dentist, nurses, carpenters, electricians, interpreters, rabbis, and other religious leaders. Refugees would also be allowed to bring personal belongings and professional tools. The officials making the selections chose "families and survivors with skills that could help run a camp in America. The first priority was refugees who had been in concentration camps and escaped."

News of the plan led relatives in the United States to advocate for their relatives in Italy. Klara Weissmann of the Bronx, New York, wrote to her member of Congress asking that her husband, Josef, then in Italy, be included among the refugees to be brought to Fort Ontario. Paul Zindwer wrote to John Pehle about his father, Nathan. "He is an Austrian National," he wrote, "who, after almost a year's internment in a German concentration camp, fled to Italy where in turn he was held as a civilian prisoner of war. . . . My brother, my sister and I, who have been in the United States for almost five years, are naturally very anxious to have him near us." Both Josef and Nathan were among those who arrived safely in Oswego.

While the plan was directed by the War Refugee Board, the details of setting up the shelter were left to the War Relocation Authority, which had been placed under the supervision of the Department of the Interior in February 1944. The War Relocation Authority was experienced in overseeing camps. It was responsible for managing the internment camps set up after Pearl Harbor to hold Japanese Americans who were forcibly relocated from their homes in the western United States.

The former army barracks at Fort Ontario were remodeled and broken up into small family apartments. Walls were painted and bathrooms updated while simple furniture—beds, chairs and tables—were put in place. All that was needed were the men, women, and children who would occupy the barracks.

— 3 —

journey to
a new life

"To share the burden of caring for refugees."
—Franklin Delano Roosevelt

O n June 20, 1944, news of the selection process
spread throughout Southern Italy. Representatives
of the War Refugee Board went to work choosing refugees for the Fort Ontario Shelter. They followed guidelines set by President Roosevelt to "include a reasonable
proportion of various categories of persecuted peoples
who have fled to Italy [and] for whom other havens of
refuge are not immediately available." In addition to
people with a cross section of skills that could make the
shelter self-sustaining, those in the greatest need were
given priority.

Refugees who hoped to be selected had to sign a Notice and Application form that presented basic but clear information about the plan. It stated, "The refugees will be brought to the United States outside of the regular immigration procedure [and] . . . they will be returned to their homes at the end of the war." Many of the nearly 3,000 people who applied did not pay attention to the fine print of the form; they only knew this was their ticket out of misery and into the United States. Some thought the rules "would never be actually enforced"—that once they arrived in the United States they would be allowed to stay permanently. Sir Clifford Heathcote-Smith, supervising the selection process, complicated matters by telling applicants, "It's only a form—pay no attention to it." Joseph Smart, the shelter director, later explained, "He was reported also to have painted a rosy picture of the luxuries to be enjoyed on the ship taking them to America (it actually was a cramped, uncomfortable transport) and at Fort Ontario."

Those selecting the 1,000 refugees were charged with creating a self-contained community. The 982 who were finally selected were a diverse group representing a cross section of society: wealthy, poor, professors, lawyers, entertainers, artists, manufacturers, teachers, clerks, and merchants. They ranged in age from infants

The Application Form

This was the document that each refugee had to sign before boarding the USAT *Henry Gibbins*:

DEPARTURE FOR THE
UNITED STATES OF AMERICA

I declare that I have fully understood the following conditions of the offer of the United States Government and that I have accepted them:

I. I shall be brought to a reception center in Fort Ontario in the State of New York, where I shall remain as a guest of the United States until the end of the war. Then I must return to my homeland.

II. There I shall live under the restrictions imposed by the American security officials.

III. No promise of any kind was given to me either in regard to a possibility of working or permission to work outside the reception center, or in regard to the possibility of remaining in the United States after the war.

IV. I declare further, since I cannot take along any valuta [foreign currency] under existing laws, that I shall accept in exchange for my valuta, the same amount in dollars, which the authorities of the United States will eventually pay me after my arrival in America.

to an 80-year-old. Among them were 192 merchants or salesmen, 27 manufacturers, 26 tailors, 9 writers, and 5 physicians.

When asked why his parents made the decision to apply, Walter Greenberg said, "We had nothing in Italy, we had no homes, it was starting anew, and I think that

Regina Gal and her children left France when the Germans arrived and made their way over the Alps to safety in Italy before being selected to come to Fort Ontario.

coming to this country meant that at least for the duration of the war there would be food and shelter and, hopefully, school and the normalities of life, and I think that's why they came."

In rapid order, army trucks picked up the selected refugees from internment camps and Rome and made their way to the port in Naples. About 75 percent of those chosen came from the internment camps in Southern Italy: Ferramonti, Bari, Santa Maria di Bagni, and Campagna. The remaining 25 percent came from Rome, where most had been living in hiding.

Manya Hartmayer was hiding in a Catholic convent in Rome. "I found myself alone in this convent, where I was, of course, protected, but in mortal danger because even there the Germans came in. They had penetrated, they had overwhelmed Italy; it was very close, every day, to be deported. I knew that. I knew that when they get me I would not come out alive." After the American Fifth Army liberated the city from the Germans on June 5, 1944, Manya filled out an application to come to Fort Ontario.

The chosen refugees boarded trucks wearing the clothes on their backs and carrying sacks or tattered suitcases containing their meager possessions. A few wore the striped pajamas they received in German concentration camps. Some children were barefoot.

Tamar Hendel

Tamar Hendel was born in Zagreb, Yugoslavia, in 1935. Her father was a textile merchant. When the Germans entered their country, her family went into hiding and ended up with relatives in Slovenia. They eventually made their way to Rovigo, Italy. One step ahead of the Nazis who took control of Italy, they went to Rome. There, her brother studied safely in a Catholic school. In 1944, when the United States liberated Southern Italy, the Hendel family signed up to come to Oswego.

Manya remembered, "A few days later I found myself on an American truck, an army truck that took me out of hell. And I joined the rest of the refugees on the *Henry Gibbins*."

The *Gibbins* was docked in Naples, Italy, where the refugees crowded into the front of the ship, while over 1,000 wounded American soldiers were packed into the stern. It would be a dangerous trip through the Mediterranean Sea and Atlantic Ocean, with German submarines and aircraft on the prowl. For protection, the *Gibbins* was part of a convoy of 16 troop and cargo ships accompanied by 13 warships. There were supposed to be 1,000 refugees, but the convoy was on a tight schedule and the *Gibbins* set sail with the 982 already on board. On either side of the *Gibbins* was another transport, each carrying German prisoners of war. In case of a German submarine attack on the convoy, the first victims would have been Germans.

When Secretary of the Interior Harold Ickes told his assistant, Dr. Ruth Gruber, of the plan, she told him, "Mr. Secretary, someone has to hold their hand. They'll be traumatized, they'll be terrified. Someone has to go over and prepare them for America." Secretary Ickes responded, "You're right. I'm going to send you. You're a young woman. You're Jewish, you speak German, you speak Yiddish. And I think this will mean as much to you as it does to me." Ickes appointed her to the rank of a "simulated general," which would save her life if she fell into enemy hands during her dangerous mission. On board the *Gibbins* and into the Oswego camp, she became the refugees' adviser, teacher, and confidant.

The two-week sea voyage was long and uncomfortable. Eva Kaufmann remembered, "It was very cramped quarters on the ship. It was made for American soldiers,

Dr. Ruth Gruber (center with military cap) poses with a group of Jewish displaced persons just arrived from Europe in 1946. Gruber accompanied the 982 refugees to Fort Ontario in 1944. When the war ended, she returned to Europe to bring other survivors to the United States.

with bunks that slept two and two and two, which is six stacked on top of each other. The other half of the ship was full of wounded soldiers. It was beastly hot."

The *Gibbins* was a military ship and operated on strict wartime regulations, including nightly blackouts while at sea. The daily schedule for the refugee group indicated when people woke up and went to bed, the time of a daily lifeboat drill, assignment of housekeeping chores, and a schedule for the two meals, breakfast and dinner. There was a daily ship's inspection. "Quarters and latrines will be policed clean and arranged as prescribed. All persons will remain on outer deck until inspection is over. . . . Bunks will remain down, blankets neatly folded and placed on one end . . . floors clean and garbage cans emptied. Latrines will be vacated by 0900, then cleaned and not used until after inspection."

Refugees were required to clean the mess hall after meals, to clean their quarters and bathrooms, and to leave their quarters every day for airing out. Many were not accustomed to manual labor and offered up excuses to avoid chores. The ship's captain advised War Refugee Board officials aboard that "the refugees know all the tricks—if they did not, many of them would not be alive today. However, we need not expect them to lay aside their tricks now."

There was one milk break for children during the afternoon. Despite cramped and overheated quarters, the travelers were overwhelmed by the amount and variety of food available. Eva Kaufmann remembered, "I never saw any kind of canned food and they had these golden peaches that looked like something out of paradise. We had lived in caves, ate nothing but boiled beans and dandelion greens, and whatever we could scrape up. And here are these wonderful golden peaches."

For safety's sake, everyone always had to wear or carry a life jacket. The refugees were warned not to throw anything out of the portholes, since "it leaves a trail for submarines." Twice during the journey, the *Gibbins* faced life-threatening dangers. Once, when a flight of German bombers flew directly overhead, army gunners on board prepared to defend the ship. Everyone breathed a sigh of relief as the planes ignored them and moved on to another target. In another scare, German submarines were detected and all on board were ordered to remain perfectly silent while the submarines posed a threat.

But the long journey also offered extended opportunities to forget the difficulties. Ruth Gruber offered popular English classes on the open deck to familiarize refugees with America. With all the talented musicians, actors, and singers on board, it did not take long for them to create and put on a show for the wounded American soldiers. The soldiers, in return, brought candy and cookies for the children. American chewing gum was an unfamiliar novelty that soon became very popular.

Above all, the refugees worried about their futures in a new country. Everyone had questions for Ruth. *What will the camp look like? Will I be able to visit my relatives in America? Can I get a job?* When told they were headed to Oswego, New York, some only heard "New York" and thought their ultimate destination was New York City.

The closest they got was a view of the city's skyline when the *Gibbins* landed at Pier 84 in Manhattan in the early evening of August 3. Ivo Lederer remembered, "If you're coming from war-time, war damaged Europe to see this enormous sight, lower Manhattan and the Statue of Liberty—I don't think there was a dry eye on deck." As the ship glided by the Statue of Liberty, one of the rabbis on board led the group on the deck in a prayer of thanksgiving. They spent the night on board while the wounded soldiers were taken off. The next morning, their difficult journey came to an end in Oswego.

The first few hours after their arrival at Fort Ontario were filled with inspections, security interviews, and getting familiar with the surroundings. Government customs officials were there to check the refugees' luggage for any illegal material. All they found inside the suitcases and packages were the few meager belongings that survived their escapes. When they realized

Military police watched over children while their parents registered. Once the procedures were completed, the army withdrew and left control of the shelter to civilians of the War Relocation Authority.

that the only tattered clothes one nine-year-old boy had were on his back, they pitched in and bought clothes and toys for him in Oswego.

The barbed-wire fence around Fort Ontario separated it from the nearby residential streets of Oswego. After local citizens watched the arrival of the newcomers, they passed cigarettes and beer to them through the fence. With limited language knowledge, some on both sides attempted conversations. Everyone was friendly and curious about the others on either side of the fence.

David Hendel remembered his arrival. "The white-washed barracks were arranged in neat rows, and for some of us conjured a strange feeling of a concentration camp. We found the building with our designated number and climbed to the second floor. To our surprise, the floor was divided into apartments, and the rooms had army cots with blankets, sheets and pillows on them. What a pleasant surprise!"

The Montiljo Family

For Moric and Mario Montiljo, arrival in America was tinged with sadness. Elia, their six-month-old baby, weakened by malnutrition, died of a fever aboard the *Henry Gibbins* on August 3. She was buried in Oswego. A flat gravestone there simply states that she DIED ON THE SHIP TO AMERICA.

To run the shelter, the War Relocation Authority called back one of their own, Joseph H. Smart, who was then on assignment in Peru. Packing up his family, he quickly moved to Oswego to assume his new responsibilities as the shelter's director. Smart was chosen because he had previous experience running a resettlement project as the director of the Japanese American

In this photo by Ansel Adams, internees at the Manzanar internment camp operated by the War Relocation Board line up for lunch. After the bombing of Pearl Harbor, Japanese Americans living on the West Coast were rounded up and sent to internment camps like this one until the war ended.

relocation program for the midwestern United States. The surprise Japanese attack on Pearl Harbor in December 1941 unleashed fear and a doubt of Japanese American loyalty. On February 19, 1942, President Roosevelt issued Executive Order 9066, ordering the internment of Japanese Americans living on the West Coast—despite the fact that there was no widespread disloyalty among these citizens. Ten camps were hastily set up in remote areas of the US that eventually held over 120,000 men, women, and children.

The day after the newcomers' arrival at Fort Ontario, the citizens of Oswego held an official welcome ceremony. The director of the War Relocation Authority, Dillon Myer, read a message from Secretary of the Interior Harold Ickes. "On behalf of the United States Government," he said, "I extend to you a hearty welcome. . . . I hope that this haven from the intolerance, suffering, and persecution that you have undergone will in some measure ease your tragic memories." There were greetings from Oswego's mayor and clergy, including Rabbi Sidney Bialik of Adath Israel Congregation representing the Jewish families of the city. Director Smart put the newcomers at ease by telling them, "Whenever there is a knock on your door, it will be a friendly one."

In response, Rabbi Mosco Tzechoval, speaking on behalf of the refugees, brought tears to the eyes of the assembled when he said that this "was the first time in more than four years that he could speak Hebrew in a public gathering without fear of a Nazi bullet."

Citizens of Oswego did their best to make the shelter residents feel welcome. With wartime shortages and rationing of manufactured goods, they held back from buying new clothing, umbrellas, and raincoats

The day after their arrival at Fort Ontario, refugees gathered for a welcoming ceremony by local dignitaries, including Oswego's mayor.

from their local merchants so the refugees could buy them. The refugees received cash grants to purchase needed clothes. An unexpected benefit to Oswego residents was the sudden availability of men's shirts, scarce across the country because of rationing. It seems that supporters of the refugees convinced the government to increase shirt availability to all in the city because of

Refugees waited patiently in lines to register and receive supplies.

the emergency clothing needs of shelter arrivals, which were a high priority. Since refugees could not leave the fort during that first month, a shopping service was set up by Oswego merchants so they could make personal purchases. With shoes much needed, local merchants set up a shoe store at the shelter and over 900 people were each fitted with a pair of shoes and two pairs of socks.

— 4 —

life behind
the fence

///

"We are in a cage, a golden cage."
—from a shelter play

///

During the 30-day quarantine period, the regfugees at Fort Ontario began to adapt to the new routines of everyday living in these very unfamiliar surroundings. But the memories of what they had just escaped remained. Still unsure whether they were truly safe, some locked their apartment doors and would open them only once the visitor was known. A reporter saw a young child in bed petting his pillow cover. His mother explained, "He's never seen sheets or a pillowcase before. I had to tell him what it was and that he was to sleep on it."

While the refugees were at sea on the *Gibbins*, workers had updated Fort Ontario's 30 wooden barracks, each two stories high with indoor and outdoor stairways. Every building contained bathing and toilet facilities for men and women. Apartments were sectioned off, plumbing installed, and a fresh coat of paint applied. Basic furniture was brought in and laundry facilities created. The rooms were small, and a major concern was a lack of privacy, since the walls were thin. First Lady Eleanor Roosevelt, who visited the shelter in September, observed, "Only the absolute necessities of life are being provided."

Additional items to make the small apartments more comfortable were donated by community and religious groups. The National Council of Jewish Women provided window curtains and new high chairs for babies. Local Camp Fire Girls collected children's books for the young refugees to read. Most refugees arrived nearly penniless, so everyone, no matter what age, was given a monthly cash allowance: $8.50 for adults (equal to $124 today), $7.00 ($102 today) for teens, and $4.50 ($66 today) for younger children. Residents who worked within the shelter received $18 ($264 today) per month.

While the refugees appreciated the abundance of food at mealtimes, what they ate fell under the same strict wartime rationing restrictions placed on all

Americans to ensure that the armed forces were amply fed and to prevent hoarding. During the war, every American received war ration books filled with stamps that, used along with money, allowed them to buy limited amounts of restricted food items such as meat, sugar, cheese, butter, and canned fish. There were

Refugees eating a meal in a dining room at Fort Ontario. They were impressed by the abundance of food.

also two mandatory meatless days each week. At the shelter, everyone ate meals together in the five dining halls. Some foods at Fort Ontario came directly from the government, while fresh vegetables, fruit, and meat were bought from local merchants. A typical menu for August 20, 1944, included:

```
Breakfast: Orange, one boiled egg, milk,
    jam, margarine, bread, and coffee
Lunch: Boiled frankfurters, sauerkraut,
    mashed potatoes, sliced tomatoes and
    cucumbers, bread and margarine, lemon
    Jell-O, and milk for the children
Dinner: Macaroni with tomato sauce,
    spinach, combination salad, bread and
    milk, and an orange
```

There were some hiccups as the shelter's residents adapted to American foods. Unfamiliar with soft American white bread, the refugees complained loudly. Shelter authorities quickly substituted dark, crusty rye bread that was more familiar to Europeans. It also took some time for the residents to get used to eating dry breakfast cereals, which they associated with animal feed. They could not forget the terrible food shortages in Europe, though, and for the first weeks at the shelter, they could not believe that there would be enough food

During the war, food, clothing, and gasoline were rationed throughout the United States to conserve supplies. All of these canned meat and fish products were rationed.

(left) Clearly posted cards in grocery stores indicated how many ration points were necessary to purchase a food item. (right) This poster was distributed to grocery stores to remind shoppers that rationing made food equally available to everyone.

for everyone. Some gorged themselves, with one man eating eight eggs at a meal.

The authorities did not expect that the refugees, underfed for months in Europe, would eat as much as combat soldiers. When they arrived "after hiding [in] the Abruzzi mountains, living in caves with 100 other people for months, they were old and haggard looking." Many had dental and optical needs that were attended to by medical professionals. While adults slowly gained back their strength, the children recuperated faster. Yet one observer noted that children over 10 years of age "don't laugh. It's hard to get them to play." Younger children bounced back much faster.

Although they were all refugees, the 982 men, women, and children came from very diverse backgrounds. They spoke a variety of languages including German, Italian, Serbo-Croatian, Yiddish, and Polish. There were 163 children under the age of 14. The names of the refugees were published in Jewish and American newspapers as they arrived. A surprising number of them had relatives already living in the United States, including brothers or sisters and sons serving in the US Army or Navy. Contact with them during the quarantine period was limited to "telephone reunions" or visits through the barbed wire fence for relatives who could journey to Oswego.

To handle the anticipated flood of telephone calls, shelter officials created a system by which every evening shelter residents could schedule calls. The very first telephone call was to the Flink family by their son, Joseph, who arrived in the United States six years earlier and was now a sergeant in the US Army. When relatives had informed him that his parents' names appeared in a newspaper, Joseph could not believe it. "Papa," he told his father over the phone, "because I hear your voice, now I believe this is true."

When a young couple, Manya Hartmayer and Ernst Breuer, wanted to marry, shelter officials did not know what to do, since both were in the United States without

legal status. Ruth Gruber came to the rescue. She arranged for them to be taken to the Oswego city clerk's office to get a marriage license. When the bride realized she would have no wedding dress to

Rabbi Sidney Bialik of Oswego's Temple Adath Israel officiated at the first wedding held at the shelter.

wear at the ceremony, Ruth telephoned her own mother in Brooklyn, who gathered up one of Ruth's dresses and crocheted a veil while on the train to Oswego. The ceremony, the first at the shelter, was conducted outdoors by Rabbi Sidney Bialik of Oswego's Adath Israel Congregation. The next day, the local newspaper provided a detailed account of the wedding, treating it as if it were a fancy high-society event.

With the birth of the couple's baby, Diana Kay, the first born in the shelter, a major legal question arose. Under the US Constitution, any child born in the United States was automatically an American citizen. But the Fort Ontario refugees were not legal immigrants and only in the country as guests of the president. Would children born in the shelter be automatic citizens of the United States? After much deliberation in Washington, the answer was yes. This created a strange situation: though all the refugees were required to return to their European homes at war's end, legally the children born at Fort Ontario would be able to stay.

When the fort was being set up to receive the refugees, a synagogue had been opened on the site, since 874 of the arrivals were Jewish. Shelter organizers soon realized that one Jewish house of worship was not enough. Around 200 Jews were Orthodox, who followed stricter religious practices than most of their fellow Jewish

Interior view of the Jewish synagogue at Fort Ontario. Furnished by outside organizations, it was one of two Jewish houses of worship at the fort to satisfy the religious needs of Orthodox and non-Orthodox Jews.

refugees. Soon, there were two synagogues at Fort Ontario. Some Jewish refugees kept kosher, observing religious rules about what food they could eat and how to prepare it. So one of the five dining halls was set up to serve completely kosher food, which was supplied by private organizations. The religious needs of the

Christian refugees were also accommodated, both in the shelter and in Oswego.

In addition to the living quarters and dining areas, there were recreation halls, a small hospital, and a theater building. Fort authorities were soon overwhelmed by offers of assistance from religious and civic organizations. To consolidate their good intentions, Director Joseph Smart formed the Coordinating Committee for Fort Ontario. Among the national groups that joined were HIAS, the National Council of Jewish Women, ORT, B'nai B'rith, the Catholic Welfare Committee, the American Friends Service Committee, and the National Refugee Service. Each was assigned a specific area of responsibility. B'nai B'rith furnished the community center building with a public address system, a radio, and a card and game room to provide a comfortable area for people to get together. Other agencies pitched in to provide services and material that the government did not provide. Eyeglasses, elective surgery, and refreshments for club meetings made life more comfortable. Perhaps the most popular offerings were the English language lessons with professional teachers who taught more than 500 refugees. Two organizations, ORT and the National Refugee Service, sponsored vocational training classes. There were courses in auto mechanics, beauty culture, and carpentry.

To provide a way to communicate with residents, the National Refugee Service provided printing equipment and supplies for a shelter newspaper, the *Ontario Chronicle*, which was published weekly from November 1944 to August 1945. The newspaper was published in

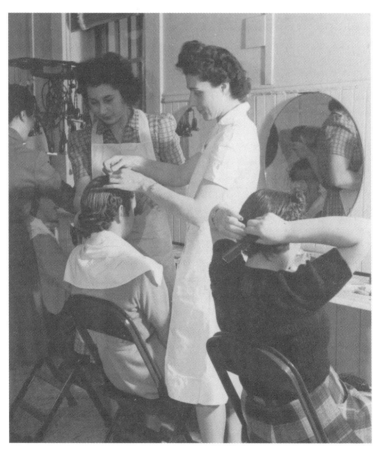

Hairstyling was one of the most popular classes offered at the shelter.

Max Sipser was a well-known European graphic artist who drew a popular weekly cartoon in the shelter's own newspaper, the *Ontario Chronicle*. He also taught art to other Fort Ontario residents.

English. The staff of writers, editors, and printers were all refugees.

Before the shelter opened, Director Smart had met with prominent Oswego citizens and formed the Oswego Citizens Advisory Committee to decide on how refugees and local citizens would interact. One of the first things created was a canteen inside the fort,

run by a local business. This became a popular destination for refugees, who could now enjoy goods like
chocolates and other merchandise not available to
them in Europe.

To allow the refugees some independence after the
quarantine period ended, they were given six-hour
passes to go into town but not beyond. This was much
appreciated, as they could walk freely down the streets,
go into shops and restaurants, and even see films in the
local theater. They enjoyed visiting the public library,
post office, and the Oswego State Teachers College
campus.

The strict rules did not stop a few daring residents
from exploring further by making use of a hole in the
fence. Several teenagers used that route to somehow
get to New York City, enjoy the sights, and return to
Oswego. One found herself on the subway and, not
knowing English, "opened my big mouth and spoke
Yiddish. And kid, I was in. All you needed to get around
New York subways was Yiddish." Elfi Strauber Hendell
remembered her mother "crawling through a hole in
the fence to board a train for New York so that she
could attend her niece's wedding. I felt my mother was
very gutsy."

When the quarantine period ended, Fort Ontario
opened for visitors. The small city of Oswego was

swamped by the arrival of American relatives and friends and overwhelmed by demands for hotel rooms. On Sunday, September 3, between 2 and 6 PM, 5,000 residents of Oswego were welcomed into the fort for an open-house program. When the fort was locked down for a month, rumors had begun circulating in the city about what was really going on behind the barbed wire

Geraldine Rossiter

Geraldine Rossiter, the girl who put her bicycle over the fence on the first day, remembered an adventure she had with two shelter friends, teenage girls. Sneaking them under the fence to a waiting automobile, Geraldine and several Oswego friends took them on a ride. "And we went to Rochester for the whole day, went to shops, went to this beautiful restaurant, and these people I knew treated them to dinner, and where the restaurant was, this nice dinner music, no dancing or anything, just nice music. And I got them back, at dark, night-time."

fence. While all Americans were living with rationing of food and clothes, some imagined that refugees
were somehow enjoying fancy surroundings and eating gourmet foods. The local newspaper editor set up
a rumor clinic to clear up misinformation. One rumor
was that refugees were buying up the limited stock of
cigarettes in Oswego stores. The newspaper responded
that it was wartime, and a cigarette shortage existed
throughout the country, not just in Oswego.

Visitors were now invited to tour several Fort Ontario
buildings, including resident housing and kitchens, and
to speak with residents. Once they saw the reality of
the sparsely furnished rooms and examined the simple
daily menus, they better understood the lives of their
new neighbors. One visitor offered a child some candy,
which he carefully put in his pocket. "Eat it, it's good,"
the visitor told him and offered him a few more pieces.
The boy put those in his pocket too. "In Europe," the
mother said, "he always saved food. We all did. It is a
habit I will have to break."

Children overcame differences faster than their parents. One local Oswego boy remembered, "Prior to
the coming of our new friends, softball, played without gloves, was our favorite outside sport whenever
the weather was favorable. However, soon after their
arrival, they began playing soccer. One by one, we

To reach downtown Oswego, shelter residents walked through this tunnel connecting to a nearby street.

opted to try this new sport and our new friends were good teachers. But we Americans suffered physically, since our 'teachers' showed no mercy during each game."

The most famous visitor to the shelter was First Lady Eleanor Roosevelt, who arrived on September 20, 1944, with her friend Elinor Morgenthau, wife of the secretary of the treasury. Roosevelt was greeted warmly with flowers and handmade gifts and toured the facilities. She took time to speak with refugees, for whom the visit was a boost in morale, and the women were guests of honor at a luncheon that afternoon. In her national newspaper column a few days later, the First Lady wrote, "Restrictions are plentiful, and there

Cultural Differences

There were cultural differences that sometimes created misunderstandings between local residents and refugees. For example, it was a custom in Europe to sit at a café for hours nursing a single cup of coffee while reading a newspaper or conversing with friends. In Europe it was also customary to haggle over prices in stores. Not in America. The wife of a State Teachers College professor remembered attending a musical concert at the fort. "The concert was fine, the performers were doing very well, but the people in the audience hissed. I was so embarrassed. I thought they should clap. . . . We learned later that hissing was a form of compliment; that was the European way."

is much work to be done around the place; but at least the menace of death is not ever-present." Although safe now in the United States, many refugees felt a lack of freedom. Living behind barbed wire, they were not allowed to work outside of the fort or travel out of Oswego to visit relatives.

It was fortunate that the refugees arrived when they did. The early August weather was warm and the breezes off Lake Ontario comforting and welcoming. Yet, by Christmas, the weather had changed dramatically. That winter, Oswego experienced the heaviest snows in years, and the temperatures plummeted. This was a shock to shelter residents who were used to the warmer climate of Southern Italy. Younger children had never seen snow before. The flimsy wooden housing offered little protection from the cold, howling winds, despite the heating systems in place.

Director Smart reported that conditions made it "impossible to maintain the people at Fort Ontario in health and safety and without actual peril to life." The Oswego fire chief advised residents to clear snow from doorways. Many residents were unable "to leave the barracks buildings even for their meals." Other residents volunteered to bring hot food from the dining halls to those unable to leave their homes. Smart observed, "Four residents suffered fractured bones during the first few days of the first storm, the winds swerving across the shelter are so strong that it is difficult for an able-bodied person to make his way against them."

First Lady Eleanor Roosevelt visiting Fort Ontario. By her side is Dr. Joseph Smart, the shelter director.

Not used to the cold Oswego winter, five shelter boys wear appropriate coats.

Despite the harsh weather conditions, life went on. There were jobs to be done. Though refugees were not allowed to work outside the shelter, and exception was made for the hiring of 50 refugees that autumn to pick apples in local orchards, since the usual workers were away in the military. Most refugees were paid to work inside the fort, where they made repairs, collected garbage, and helped with kitchen work. During the cold winter, unloading coal from trains and delivering the fuel to the barracks was unpleasant but necessary. Likewise, keeping the snow-swept roads clear was another challenge. Many residents, unaccustomed to manual labor, tried to avoid work assignments. A resident committee was formed to ensure that enough workers were on hand at all times. When it became obvious that there weren't enough men and women physically able to do all the work, outside workers were hired.

To fairly assign all able-bodied residents, a rotation schedule was created that evenly distributed the various chores. A writer for the *Ontario Chronicle* wrote with good humor about his assignment to the garbage detail. "The garbage is an interesting material," he reported, "reflecting the spirit of our residents. Some barracks are very intellectual and their garbage is chiefly composed of newspapers with the ONTARIO CHRONICLE on the honor roll. Others have a more materialistic mind with empty tobacco packages, biscuit boxes, tins, etc."

There was also time for socializing, learning, and enjoyment. There were card games, concerts, and lectures to attend. There were courses on American home life, English conversation, and arts and crafts, and even

Most residents could not work outside Fort Ontario but were expected to work within the shelter. Here several are working in a kitchen.

a class on American square dancing. Exercise classes were also popular: ping pong, volleyball, and shuffleboard competed with a weight reduction class "to keep the figure well proportioned," given the amount of food available. The State Teachers College invited residents to teas and receptions where shelter artists met with school professors. Teachers from the college delivered lectures at the shelter. The local newspaper reported, "Listening to the lectures given in English, and

Young people found ways to meet and have fun at the shelter.

participating in the discussion also help the advanced students of English to improve their knowledge and use of English."

One popular event was a 20-week lecture series on "The Culture of America." Residents were curious about the country in which they were now living, even though they were supposed to return to Europe at the end of the war. Among topics presented were "Manners and Customs," "United States Form of Government," "Art in America,'" and "Contributions to Science."

As time went on, lives of the residents began to mirror those outside Fort Ontario—though one exception remained. With travel restricted, mealtimes scheduled, and hours outside the shelter limited, one resident explained, "they possessed everything but the one thing they wanted most—freedom." Walter Greenberg remembered, "I felt deceived. I felt that I should have been free. I mean, I felt wonderful. I had doctors. I had nurses. I had food. . . . Oswegonians were very kind. . . . What good is it to have all the amenities of life if one still isn't free?"

The local superintendent of schools, Charles E. Riley, invited teachers from the area to visit Fort Ontario and teach English to the adults. One of the teachers, Frances Brown, fondly recalled the personal friendships that developed between teachers and students. Brown often invited her students to her home; the students enjoyed being inside an American home.

Members of the local Christ Episcopal Church stepped forward to "be neighborly, friendly, decent, Christian and democratic" to the shelter's young people. They invited the refugee teens to parties at the church and, in turn, asked them to tell congregants about their experiences and hopes for the future.

Forty-one residents asked permission to serve in the US military. Their request was denied by the acting secretary of war, who wrote, "It is my opinion that it would be incompatible with the conditions under which these aliens have been given refugee shelter in this country to permit any of them, otherwise eligible, to enter the Armed Forces of the United States."

Oswegonians were also treated to public performances by talented refugees, some of whom were celebrated actors, singers, and entertainers in their home countries. Adults and children alike eagerly anticipated the celebration of Christmas and Hanukkah 1944. That first Christmas at the fort was marked by a community Christmas tree, carols, and concerts. A national Christmas broadcast from the shelter on the NBC radio network featured noted reporter Dorothy Thompson and a newly created Fort Ontario choir singing holiday songs.

Jewish and Christian residents joined to celebrate each other's holidays. There were parties and decorations, and Santa Claus made an appearance to distribute gifts. The Oswego High School chorus serenaded residents. An editorial in the *Ontario Chronicle* expressed everyone's feelings that "we are fed till the end of the war and are well cared for, as everybody must admit. We are here not only protected from material want and misery, but we can find here moral relief." Shelter director Joseph Smart told the residents, "Whether our guiding light is the star of David or the star of Bethlehem, we are united in the conviction that right shall prevail; and that all men in freedom under law, can live together in personal dignity and love."

Confinement to the shelter had tragic moments as well. For the ill and aged with relatives in the United States who could take care of them, there was only loneliness, since shelter residents could not travel beyond Oswego. Dr. Nathan Zindwer had family in the country, including his son, Paul, who had written to

Free to practice their religion after escaping Europe, this Jewish family lights a Hanukkah menorah in their shelter apartment.

the War Refugee Board on his behalf, and a daughter who was a doctor in Boston, yet he died alone in the fort among strangers in August 1945 and was buried in Oswego's Riverside Cemetery.

For the children, however, there was a different experience.

— 5 —

like other children

"Foreigners are real people."
—Naomi Jolles

The major responsibility of the War Relocation Authority at Fort Ontario was to provide refugees with shelter, food, and medical care. Yet with the realization that 232 of the shelter residents would be school-age children, something had to be done about their education. Most of the younger children had never attended school. For older children, it had been years since many were in a formal classroom. Walter Greenberg remembered that as a 13-year-old, "I was a man in a world that I had seen so much and experienced so much. I think we all were too old for our age."

Student numbers in the public schools of Oswego had decreased in 1944, leaving classroom space that could be filled by shelter children without hiring additional teachers. Member organizations on the Coordinating Committee for Fort Ontario paid for additional expenses. These included textbooks, school supplies, lunches, appropriate clothing for students (especially during the harsh Oswego winters), and transportation costs.

Appreciative of being able to continue their education, shelter students pose proudly in front of Oswego High School.

Dr. Ralph Faust, principal of Oswego High School, took the first steps to help absorb shelter students into the Oswego schools. Toward the end of August, before the beginning of the school year, Dr. Faust visited Fort Ontario often to encourage high school–age shelter teens to enroll in Oswego High School. With the young people eager to resume their education, the principal interviewed each one to find out how much knowledge they had of science, math, and English in order to place them in appropriate classes.

Peter Sommerburg

Fourteen-year-old Peter Sommerburg was born in Hamburg, Germany. He was in the shelter with his mother, two sisters, and two brothers. He did not know if his father, left behind in Germany, was alive or dead. The family spent years in Italy, where Peter began learning English. He had not attended school for six years when he reached Fort Ontario and became a first-year student at Oswego High School.

The day before school started, Dr. Faust gave the shelter students a tour of the building to familiarize them with their new school. He later recalled showing the students the shop class floor: "As they looked into these shop doors, I can distinctly remember them saying—hearing the words over the babble of German—'magnifique!'" Years later, one of those students, Ivo Lederer, recalled, "The teachers in the high school were fantastic; I still have something I made under Mr. Crabtree, our shop teacher." At a welcoming assembly the next day, Dr. Faust introduced 40 shelter students to the school. At the end of the school year, Dr. Faust made it possible for six of the shelter students to take the New York State exams, which permitted them to graduate from Oswego High School and participate in the graduation exercises.

Younger children attended either a parochial school, one of two Oswego public schools—School Number 2 or the Fitzhugh Park School—or the Campus Elementary School at the Oswego State Teachers College. When Dr. Ralph Swetman, the college president, was asked to accept the students, he responded, "We shall be very happy to have them with us."

Their first day of school was as surprising to the local students as to their new classmates. The Oswego children were impressed that the newcomers were able

For the youngest children, volunteers organized a nursery school and playgroups to provide fun activities.

Children were kept busy with a variety of activities.

to speak multiple languages. Yet it was hard for refugees to forget where they came from. Walter Greenberg remembered that the shelter students, who had

Fourth-grade refugee children at the Campus School of Oswego State Teachers College.

experienced terrible things in Europe, wanted "to be happy, and carefree like them, but they can't understand why we are the way we are." One Oswego student later remembered seeing a first-grade shelter boy doodling warplanes and air battles with bullets flying.

From their first interactions across the shelter fence, the refugee children knew that the boys and girls on the other side were like them. But it would take a little time for the newcomers to be totally accepted as equals. At the teachers college school, puzzled refugee children approached their teacher to ask what language the other children were speaking. With their knowledge of languages, they knew it was not English. It turned out that to show their new classmates they too could speak more than one language, the Oswego children were speaking in Pig Latin.

The new students were a positive influence on their American classmates. After not being in school for years or never, the shelter children took education seriously. When one local student made fun of Ernest Spitzer from Vienna for being so committed to learning, the refugee boy answered, "In prison camp I was too hungry to study, I have forgotten much. Don't mind me, but I must make it up." A local high school student said, "At first a lot of kids laughed at them for being grinds, but it certainly made you feel small." A school admin-

Learning School Rules

Shelter parents received a message from the Oswego School District introducing them to the ways of American schools:

Your children are now attending the public schools in a new and strange land. Many of them are not familiar with democratic procedures and all of them are naturally unfamiliar with the American school system.

We are anxious to do all we can for your children but we need your immediate cooperation in helping your children make a rapid adjustment to our way of doing things. We would therefore urge you to impress upon your children the desirability of a rapid adjustment to the American pattern of behavior in the school, on the playground, and on the streets.

This is a sample of the rules for students, most of whom had never been in a school:

Obey the teacher—she is your friend and wishes to help you all she can. . . .

Be quiet in school. You cannot learn if you are creating a disturbance. . . . American boys and girls are taught not to attract attention to themselves by being noisy, disobedient, or uncooperative. . . .

Do not lay your hands on one another. Do not push or shove other pupils and do not run in the school building. . . .

Do not hum, stamp, whistle, or mumble in the classroom. . . .

Speak English in the school at all times. . . .

In going to and from school walk on the sidewalks.

The list concluded with these words from Dr. Charles Riley, the superintendent of schools:

We are happy to share our school facilities with you and we know you will wish to show your gratitude by observing all of our rules, regulations and customs.

istrator said, "They did inspire our own youngsters. They were very careful about citizenship, politeness, and they were very anxious to conform to the rules and regulations. . . . I think they have greatly stimulated our own boys and girls." In return, refugee student Edith Bronner said, it was the "first normal teenage life we ever had." The refugees created increased interest in geography and history—especially American history—

Refugee students studying in an Oswego High School classroom. They were especially focused on their studies and served as a positive influence on their fellow Oswego students.

in their classrooms. The city librarian was pleased by frequent visits by refugee students and an increased borrowing of foreign dictionaries by local students.

The shelter children were not kept in separate classrooms but divided up among the other students. Some students were bused, while those at the high school and School Number 2 walked to and from school. While local children went home for lunch and then returned to school, the shelter children remained behind and ate lunch together, since the trip back to the fort was too difficult, especially during the snowy winter months.

In a class where the students were discussing Thanksgiving, one of the refugee children asked who the Pilgrims were. The teacher answered, "They were people who came here to find freedom of religion." "Oh, then," the student replied, "we're just like the Pilgrims." That got the local students to thinking that since everyone liked the Pilgrims, who were refugees, then their classmate refugees were welcome, too.

Although they had language difficulties at first, it did not take long for them to get good grades, with many on the honor roll. The Fitzhugh Park School's principal, Virginia Dean, later recalled, "How quickly those young people, who were certainly far above average in intelligence—that was one of the things that I noticed—could pick up the English."

Putting Emotions into Words

Principal Faust later shared an essay written by a 15-year-old refugee student at Oswego High School, Ralph Kuznitzki, which revealed the student's progress not only with the English language but also with his inner feelings:

The fresh and rather cold morning breeze blew directly in my face; making my ears and the tip of my nose red. I had passed the houses which protected me against it, and now I was crossing a wet lawn. I hurried to pass it. But when I arrived at the next block of houses, I noticed that a small part of it had come along with me. It was stuck in my shoe, that small flower. After having picked it up, I was about to throw it away, when I suddenly came to think of a strange fact. How greatly likely was the flower's life with mine! It may be a stupid idea, but there is something true with it.

Within weeks of school beginning, a shelter student at the Fitzhugh Park School was elected class president. Teachers were amazed at the eagerness of their new students to learn and absorb American culture. Dr. Ralph Swetman, president of the State Teachers College, said his shelter students "fitted in very nicely with our children and before long it was hard to tell them apart when you would go into the room."

Friendships were common between local students and shelter students, both in and out of school. Since high school students had permission to spend time outside of the fort, they enjoyed visiting the homes of local friends, ice cream shops, and restaurants. Back in the

Refugee youths eat lunch together in a shelter dining room.

fort, students had time to do their homework, perform chores, and socialize.

An unusual opportunity for boys was the establishment of a Boy Scout troop within Fort Ontario. Troop 28 was the idea of Howard Clark, the scoutmaster of an already established troop in the area. He worked within sight of the shelter and every day saw the children on the other side of the fence. He decided that a scout troop inside was a way to give shelter boys a classic American experience.

Children and leaders of the Fort Ontario Cub Scout group. Scouting was a popular activity for boys and girls that helped them connect to American life.

Refugee children learning.

For the boys, this was an entirely new but meaningful experience. They welcomed the attention given to them by Mr. Clark. The boys proudly wore their Boy Scout uniforms, which they paid for by collecting tons of newspapers and selling them for scrap to be used in the war effort. They enjoyed typical scout activities, especially hiking. Mr. Clark remembered, "They built their fire out there, they cooked, they camped, they hiked, they earned their badges."

"I can't get over their enthusiasm," Mr. Clark later said, "I can see them now, so eager and so happy to be here." Walter Greenberg remembered, "It was a good happy time. . . . I was very proud of my uniform coming from a kind of place where uniforms meant terror." Not to be outdone, Cub Scout and Girl Scout troops soon followed.

Nine young people who had completed high school in Europe were accepted into the State Teachers College to continue their education. Their tuition and other expenses were paid for by agencies of the Coordinating Committee. In return, they were expected to work a few hours weekly at the shelter. Although none of them desired to become teachers, they could take other courses such as English, history, sociology, and literature. Two brothers at the college, Aca and Rajko Margulis, who had studied medicine at the University of Belgrade in Yugoslavia, both gained admission to Harvard Medical School based on their high marks in Oswego. However, like other shelter residents whose future in the United States was unclear, the brothers were bound by Fort Ontario's rules, and they were not allowed to leave Oswego to attend Harvard.

The Margulis Brothers

On leaving the shelter to return to Yugo-slavia at the end of the war, the Margulis brothers sent college president Dr. Ralph Swetman a thank-you letter. "Leaving this country," they wrote, "we desire to express to you once more our deep gratitude for all the kindness you have showed us. We shall never forget the friendly atmosphere we enjoyed while attending the Oswego State Teachers College. . . . We know that we have sincere friends in Oswego who tried their best, as you did to help us. It was really a pleasure to study in a school led by you." They eventually returned to the United States to attend Harvard Medical School. Both achieved their lifelong ambitions to became physicians.

— 6 —

to stay or
not to stay

"At the end of the war, they will
be returned to their homelands."
—Franklin Delano Roosevelt

Despite the refugees' feelings of thankfulness and
safety, they were bothered by the restrictions
placed on their lives. One of the most popular songs
within the shelter was "Don't Fence Me In." Ironically,
that same song was also popular with the German
prisoners of war placed in 500 camps throughout the
United States, several within reach of Oswego.

While the number of refugees at the shelter was
too little and too late, given the millions of Jews and
others already dead in Europe, no one could forget the

While only 982 refugees received safe haven in the United States, over 400,000 German soldiers were brought to camps throughout the country as prisoners of war, where they could work for wages while waiting for the war to end. Shelter residents thought the German prisoners had more freedom than they had in the United States.

large number of German soldiers brought to this country. While shelter residents were not allowed to work outside the fort, the prisoners of war were employed—under supervision, of course—in fields, mills, and factories, replacing American soldiers who were overseas.

As the war in Europe was winding down, residents of the shelter continued with their lives behind the Fort Ontario fence. In many respects, life inside the fort resembled a typical American town. Most of the adults

Children playing outside at the fort.

worked within Fort Ontario and the children attended school. After a while, they wore clothes that mirrored the dress of people outside the fence. Except for the fact that they ate their meals in dining halls rather than in the kitchens and dining rooms of private homes, there was little to distinguish them from American families. The only thing they lacked was freedom. Walter Greenberg remembered, "There was a fence, and that fence separated me from the outside world."

All the while, the refugees worried about what would happen to them when the war ended. In the back of their minds was the paper they had signed before they boarded the USAT *Henry Gibbins* in Naples, which said that they "will be returned to their homelands." A reporter noted, "They fretted ceaselessly. Minor events took on exaggerated meaning. Rumors were rampant. Nerves were rubbed raw."

Shelter director Smart put it this way. "They seem gay and cheerful at their parties. However, our social workers tell us that in the privacy of their living quarters you can learn of their despondency." Many felt they had less freedom in America than in Italy. Some had relatives living in the United States they could not visit. They knew of the shortage of factory workers, yet they were not allowed to work, even while German prisoners of war did. Above all hovered the question of their uncertain futures. Legally, they were now people without a country. Most wanted to remain in the United States. Miriam Sommerburg told a reporter, "I will never go back to Germany. I can't go back." Another refugee, Fredi Baum, said, "I believe there is more of a future in America than in Yugoslavia because you will have a normal life here."

A shelter resident, Ernst Wolff, wrote a personal and heartfelt appeal to First Lady Eleanor Roosevelt, whom he had met when she visited Fort Ontario. In less than perfect English, he implored her, "Be our lawyer, than

A youth group dance at Fort Ontario was one of many kinds of social activities for young and old in the shelter.

[then] your voice will be heart [heard] and not only we, we will be thankfull [thankful] all user [our] life and only we will bless you, but to our children and children of our children."

Sadness gripped Fort Ontario when news arrived of President Roosevelt's death on April 12, 1945. The refugees felt a close relationship with the president who had allowed them to find safety in the United States.

The residents gathered at a memorial ceremony on April 14, attended by Director Smart and his family. Rabbi Mosco Tzechoval officiated along with Rabbi Sydney Bialik. Fredi Baum spoke on behalf of all the refugees. "We, residents of this shelter, too mourn sincerely and with all our hearts this wonderful, noble, and great man. We still gratefully remember the visit of Eleanor Roosevelt, who so thoughtfully revived our morale." The next day, another memorial service was held at Rabbi Bialik's synagogue in Oswego, which was attended by a group of shelter residents. Attention now turned to the new president, Harry S. Truman.

The war in Europe ended with Germany's surrender on May 8, 1945. A small percentage of the refugees expressed the desire to return to their home countries. In June, 13 returned to Yugoslavia. In total, 69 refugees would return to their homelands. But the vast majority realized that they had no homes to return to. Their families were dead, their former businesses gone; despite the agreement they had signed in Naples, they wanted to remain in the United States.

Leading citizens of Oswego took on the refugees' case and sent a petition to Congress and to President Truman, urging that the refugees be released and allowed to legally apply for admission to the United States under the existing immigration laws. The petition stated that the shelter had "taken on the psychological aspect of a prison and urged that the refugees be given their freedom and be permitted to decide for themselves where their future homes should be." Another petition signed by 100 famous people including Albert Einstein, Eleanor Roosevelt, and former governor of New York Herbert Lehman, urged the government to allow Fort Ontario residents "to live and work wherever they choose in the United States." The petition continued, "While Americans are fighting to establish freedom and human dignity throughout the world, it is scarcely to be tolerated that anti-Nazi refugees should be confined against their will."

The shelter's director, Joseph Smart, also supported the refugees and urged the War Relocation Authority to loosen the strict travel rules, unfortunately without success. Residents were upset that they could not at least travel outside of Oswego to visit relatives. "Why should the residents—their number is not too high—not be authorized to see their relatives at their homes?" a newspaper editorial questioned. Many rumors swirled about the shelter, including one that it was about to be closed and the residents shipped to a United Nations camp in North Africa.

Concerned with these rumors and that there seemed to be no solution to solving the problem of the residents' futures, Smart resigned his position as director effective May 15. His stated reason was "so that I will have freedom and can devote all my interest and energy to the cause of freedom for this people free of governmental restrictions." In a letter to Rabbi Eliezer Silver, Smart wrote, "My sole objective is that the Fort Ontario refugees be given status of immigrants, and I will not be satisfied with less."

Mr. Smart was succeeded by acting director Malcolm Pitts. Smart's family remained in Oswego and

Miriam Sommerburg (right) was an accomplished sculptor and artist. Here she proudly shows a bust she created of Joseph Smart, the shelter director.

continued to spend time at the shelter supporting the residents. Smart himself formed a committee known as Friends of Fort Ontario Guest-Refugees to petition the president and government leaders, becoming its executive director. "It is important that plans be made immediately for the future," he told a gathering of refugees at the fort before he left, "and this will be my main task working in cooperation with private and official agencies."

Smart told shelter residents, "I propose to enlist all the powerful and responsible support I can in creating a favorable attitude in Congress." His encouraging words "received enthusiastic and unanimous applause of a deeply moved audience." The residents understood that from the beginning of their stay at the shelter, Smart "has always shown the best comprehension for our sorrow and joys."

An editorial written by a refugee in the *Ontario Chronicle* stated, "The speech of Mr. Smart made it clear that our only and overshadowing problem remains the recognition of us as immigrants by the American authorities. . . . We are no beggars . . . a return to their homelands in Europe signifies no more nor less than a death warrant."

Smart had support from a long list of private agencies that contributed to the well-being of the refugees and would continue to stand up for them now. Included were the Oswego Citizens Advisory Committee, the National Refugee Service, HIAS, the National Council of Jewish Women, B'nai B'rith, the YMCA, and the American Committee for Christian Refugees. Smart's new organization also enlisted support from important political and religious leaders.

The first to respond were influential Oswegonians, including Dr. Ralph Swetman, president of the State

Hadesa Sochaczewska

Hadesa Sochaczewska was a Polish citizen who escaped to Italy, where she was interned at the Ferramonti camp for three and a half years. After arrival at Fort Ontario she learned that her immediate family had been killed by the Nazis. "So, I am alone," she said. "I think I will never get rid of the complex of inferiority. I envy everybody who has a family, home and country. . . . There is no road back to my country. . . . How long have I still to wait until I will start my individual personal life."

Teachers College, and Edwin Waterbury, publisher of the local newspaper. In a letter to Eleanor Roosevelt asking for her public support, Smart wrote, "Here is an opportunity to maintain the American traditions of fair play and generous treatment of the oppressed, for people who are already in our land who literally have no place else to go." The First Lady pledged her support.

The plight of the refugees was debated across the country. One woman stated in a letter to the editor of the *New York Daily News,* "These refugees came in under Presidential directive—a shady business in itself—and they agreed to the terms of that special entry. We should insist that they abide by their agreement and return as quickly as possible to their native countries."

Similar letters appeared in local Oswego newspapers and upset shelter residents. The acting director of Fort Ontario sent a letter to calm the residents stating, "It is the American way to discuss public issues in all types of public forums. Each individual has a right to express himself. . . . While it is probably true that many of the unfriendly letters in the newspapers have been exaggerated and misleading, I should like to urge all residents to avoid doing anything in Oswego (or anywhere else) which might cause any one to write an unfriendly letter."

Young people at the Fort Ontario Shelter enjoyed the opportunities to socialize with one another.

There was also much support for the refugees. A typical newspaper editorial stated, "Driven from their homes years before they were brought here, these people now have no place to go in Europe. True, they are the lucky ones of millions who are no better off, but the United States can afford to be generous for these few who are here, without committing itself to letting down the bars against immigration generally."

Individuals made their opinions known to government officials. Irma Shapleigh of Baltimore, Maryland, wrote directly to the secretary of state. "Surely it seems as if the tradition of our country as an asylum for the oppressed should be upheld at this time," she said. She further urged the government to have "our immigration laws altered now to admit at least some of those Jews who are still alive in Europe."

The War Refugee Board was "besieged by pressure groups which want to keep the refugees here." In Congress, the chair of the House Committee on Immigration and Naturalization, Congressman Samuel

Else Regenhardt

Dr. Else Regenhardt was a prominent physician in Vienna, Austria. When the Germans entered Austria in 1938, she fled to Italy. For the next six years, she survived by moving from place to place in Italy under harsh conditions before coming to Fort Ontario. "I'm very satisfied here," she said, "It's like a heaven. Now soon, I will be myself again." As to returning to her native Austria, she bitterly said she was "thrown out like a dog. I will never go back there; never."

Dickstein of New York, led the fight to permit the Fort Ontario refugees to remain in the United States. On June 25 and 26, 1945, he brought members of a subcommittee to the fort, where they held an official congressional "Investigation of Problems Presented by Refugees at Fort Ontario Refugee Shelter."

On the first day, members of Congress heard from officials of the War Refugee Board, from shelter officials, and from residents about their experiences in Europe and in the fort. The purpose was to strengthen the case for allowing the refugees the opportunity to remain in the United States. The first witness was General William O'Dwyer, executive director of the War Refugee Board, who provided detailed historical information about the shelter. When asked his opinion about returning the refugees to Europe, he argued that "they be permitted to stay in the United States until the United Nations have settled the problem of displaced persons."

The next witnesses were members of the shelter's Boy Scout troop. Dressed in their uniforms, they stood proudly in front of the committee and recited the Boy Scout Oath. Then they were individually asked about their lives and if they wanted to remain in the United States and, if necessary, serve in the US military. Their nearly unanimous response was, "Yes." Mr. Dickstein then said, "I think you would make a good scout, and a good soldier and a good citizen."

Ruth Gruber, who had led the refugees from Italy to Oswego, and other Department of the Interior officials provided the members of Congress with an overview of conditions in the shelter and the thoughts of the residents about their futures. Dr. Gruber said, "The people are completely democracy-conscious. The children listen to the radio, they go to the movies, they study the Constitution, they bring the whole spirit of the Bill of Rights home to their parents. The parents are just as conscious of American democracy as the children are."

The next day the committee heard from educational leaders, Oswego officials, and shelter residents themselves. When asked if the refugee children could become loyal Americans, Dr. Ralph Swetman of the State Teachers College responded, "There would be no question on my part in regard to that; as far as these youngsters are concerned I know what they are, and I think they would fall in beautifully. . . . I think they would become pretty good Americans." When asked, "You think they should stay here and continue their studies?" the principal of the School Number 2, Susan Donovan, responded, "I think they should be allowed to remain." Dr. Ralph Faust, the Oswego High School principal, proudly told the committee that eight of the shelter students had qualified for the National Honor Society, while another teacher added, "These boys are of the finest I have ever had in my homeroom."

The Oswego police chief was asked if there were any signs of trouble between the refugees and city residents. His response was "No, sir; we haven't had any trouble with these refugees in our city." The editor of a local newspaper spoke of the positive contributions the refugees made to the city. "They are a very talented group," he said. "There is more talent in this group than there is in all of Oswego together."

Finally, the committee heard from several refugees, who dramatically described the hardships they endured in Europe and their hopes for the future. They listened to Rosa Mosauer, who had two sons serving in the US Army, and Jacob Charasch, whose two sons served in the US Merchant Marine. They also heard about the Margulis brothers, who had been accepted to Harvard Medical School but would not be permitted to attend. The hearing ended with Chairman Dickstein saying, "We have been here for two days and have talked with these people, and I think we have a complete picture."

Mr. Dickstein's subcommittee reported back to the full committee in Washington, which issued a resolution on July 6 calling on the State and Justice Departments to see if it made sense to return the refugees to

Dr. Ernst Flatau

Dr. Ernst Flatau was a successful Berlin law-yer. After Kristallnacht in November 1938, he was arrested and sent to the Sachsen-hausen concentration camp for four months. Upon his release, he began the process of applying for an American visa at the Ameri-can consulate in Berlin. His mother was American, as were his wife's parents, so he didn't think he would have a problem. But, whether on purpose or not, he soon became snared in an inescapable paperwork trap. Just when he gathered necessary affida-vits, sworn official statements of support from American sponsors, Dr. Flatau, his wife, and their twin sons were deported to Prague, Czechoslovakia.

Dr. Flatau continued to work with the American consulate there, but Prague was soon occupied by the Nazis, and the family escaped to Italy and the Ferramonti refugee camp. The American consul in Naples transferred the Flatau files from Berlin and Prague. "I was to call at the American Consulate in Naples in January 1941," Flatau later said, "to apply formally for the immigration visa but at the time the consul told us we would have to renew the affidavits and to bring a statement about the income of the sponsors. When the affidavits came back, the American consulates in Italy were closed." The Flatau family spent the last 10 months in Rome before they heard about the possibility to come to America aboard the *Henry Gibbins*.

their homelands. All the attention to their problems lifted the refugees' spirits that summer as their activities at the shelter continued. The school year ended on a positive note, with many of the children receiving honors, which brought pride to them and their families.

With a limited staff, however, the shelter administration faced difficulties in organizing summer activities for children and adults. An energetic group from the American Friends Service Committee arrived at the fort and came to their rescue. Run by the Society of Friends, a religious denomination also known as the

Quakers, the committee brought their expertise in creating educational and recreational activities to the residents of all ages. Taking up residence in a house at the fort, they became completely accepted by the refugee population and provided much-needed programming that kept residents involved all summer.

The theater and musical groups were also active, and the artwork of talented residents went on display at a Syracuse art museum (although no residents could attend, since the city was beyond the allowable travel range). Over the course of a month, 5,000 Oswego residents visited a special art exhibit at Fort Ontario put on by refugees. Shelter musicians entertained at community events in Oswego and raised money for the Red Cross.

Across the country, people considered the fate of the refugees. New York City Mayor Fiorello La Guardia wrote, "The present confinement of these people, by whatever name it may be called or under what good intentions they were brought here, is nonetheless a concentration camp. I feel that something should be done about it."

On July 15, 1945, reporter Robert St. John used his popular NBC radio program to describe the plight of the Fort Ontario Shelter residents. "It is up to Congress now, because a congressional committee is investigating

Artwork created by Miriam Sommerburg for the program cover of the operetta *The Golden Cage*.

the case. The fate of these 969 people who have lived behind steel wire (getting such a bad opinion of these United States) may well depend on whether you care. I hope you do."

He asked his nationwide listeners to share their opinions. Of the over 500 who did, 79 percent favored allowing the refugees to stay; 17 percent opposed.

One supporter said, "In the name of all that America stands for, these people should be allowed to remain here and given every opportunity and encouragement to become American citizens." Another wrote, "If we don't give these refugees full freedom, the very intolerances we are fighting sneaks [sic] in behind the ranks of our men."

The refugees made their own opinion known to President Harry Truman and other government officials. On August 3, 1945, one year after their arrival at Fort Ontario, they sent a letter that stated, "We would like to present . . . the heart-felt request that all those members of our community who have lost every tie to their homelands through the loss of their closest relatives and friends, occupations and fortunes, and who for this reason and persecuted by the nightmare of the past, can never again live in any country poisoned by the Nazi ideology, will be granted an opportunity for a new home and reconstruction of their lives in your great country."

On October 22, representatives of all the private agencies who supported the refugees at Fort Ontario also wrote to President Truman. "This letter . . . is addressed to you jointly by the Catholic, Jewish, Protestant and non-sectarian welfare agencies which have been concerned with the care of these unfortunate people during the 14 months that they have been in this country. . . . It is self-evident," they wrote, "that the government cannot continue indefinitely to support these 900 persons at Fort Ontario . . . we believe that under the existing immigration laws of the United States, it is possible for you to take action that will make possible the release of these refugees . . . and their resettlement in the United States."

As shelter residents awaited a second winter in Oswego, they were discouraged by the lack of success in resolving their situation. While they worried, others in Washington were deciding their futures.

— 7 —

when the gates opened

"Now all is behind me, and a new life
has started." —former shelter resident

Behind the scenes in Washington, DC, government agencies studied the situation as public opinion grew in favor of the refugees. The Friends of Fort Ontario committee urged the government to "give the guest refugees at Fort Ontario their immediate freedom to live and work wherever they choose in the United States; and regularize, as quickly as possible, the status of those who normally would have been eligible for immigration."

Finally, on December 22, 1945, President Truman issued a statement about people around the world who were displaced by the war. He ordered the admission into the country of displaced persons and refugees under existing immigration laws. The president made a special reference to the shelter refugees in Oswego, allowing those who wished to stay to become legal immigrants. "This is the opportunity," the president said, "for America to set an example for the rest of the world in cooperation toward alleviating human misery." He made the point that "if these persons were now applying for admission to the United States most of them would be admissible under the immigration laws."

Knowing that their futures in the United States were now guaranteed, the refugees at Fort Ontario celebrated New Year's 1946 in especially festive fashion. There were two parties, one featuring a play and the other a dance and special music.

To become a legal immigrant to the United States, a person had to obtain a visa outside the country. "In the circumstances," President Truman wrote, "it would be inhumane and wasteful to require these people to go all the way back to Europe merely for the purpose of applying there for immigration visas and returning to the United States." The president's plan allowed refugees to claim available unused quota numbers. Because immigration to the United States had been virtually at a standstill during the war, shelter residents could apply for visas using their respective home countries' unused immigration slots.

A simple plan was devised using the American consulate at Niagara Falls, Canada. After examinations by officials of the Immigration and Naturalization Service at the fort, the refugees would be bused in small groups across the nearby Canadian American border to receive visas and then move on to their new homes. Refugees thought it funny that, in order to enter America, one

Good News

Geraldine Rossiter was visiting in the shelter when residents heard the news. "It was activity like Christmas or something. 'We're gettin' packed up, we're gonna go, gee we're gonna go there and then we can go anywhere we want to.' Certainly they didn't have it easy, but they never would have been able to afford to do any of these things, as far as I could see, at all, unless the Jewish organizations throughout the United States had contributed to this cause."

had to leave it first. While residents busied themselves with final preparations, several farewell parties were held with joyful singing and dancing.

The National Refugee Service had the major responsibility, together with other private agencies, of placing the residents. Refugees with relatives or friends in the United States were encouraged to resettle in those communities where they would have a support team ready. Others were helped to select communities where local agencies stood ready to help with housing and employment. The 18 months in the shelter provided them with experiences to succeed in their new homes. They had learned to speak and understand English and had become familiar with American customs, and although Oswego was a small city, their interactions there gave them confidence to face their new lives in the United States.

The refugee children who attended Oswego schools were fully prepared to continue with their education wherever they settled. Oswego's superintendent of schools, Dr. Charles Riley, wrote, "All in all it was a delightful experience. There wasn't a single unfortunate incident to spoil the picture. Our only regret is that we could not keep these children until they all graduated from high school. I am absolutely certain, however, that they are off to an excellent start and they

Young children developed a daily routine returning to Fort Ontario from school.

will adjust themselves immediately in any school system they enter."

At 6 AM on Wednesday, January 17, 1946, the first group of 92 refugees boarded three buses and was driven across the border to the American consulate. The consul, George S. Graves, presented each one with a preprepared visa document. They then crossed back into the United States as legal residents. One of the refugees, Jacob Kahn, told a reporter, "It's wonderful! People have been wonderful to me. Now I'm looking forward to becoming an American citizen. That will be the gladdest day of my life." The new American residents were treated to a hot meal at Temple Beth El in Buffalo and helped on their way to new homes by workers from HIAS and the National Refugee Service, who made all the arrangements for travel and baggage shipments.

Until their departures, some were housed in a small hotel rented by the National Refugee Service or in private homes of Buffalo residents. Many had relatives or friends in the United States and went to be with them. Others were welcomed by Jewish communities across the country. The American Committee for Christian Refugees and the Catholic Committee for Refugees developed resettlement plans for their own clients.

The frequent bus departures to the Canadian border took place in the early morning so the visas could be granted the same day. Those departing gathered between 4 and 5 AM for coffee and doughnuts while their neighbors and friends came out to say goodbye and wish them well. Between January 17 and February 5, 1946, the remaining shelter residents met with the US consul across the border in Canada, who gave each of them the long-awaited document by which they could reenter the United States, 765 as permanent residents and 134, who didn't qualify for a quota assignment that month, as temporary residents.

By mid-February, former shelter residents were resettled in 68 communities in 20 states by social workers from the private agencies who worked closely with the War Relocation Authority. "Arrangements were made for the travel and reception of each family group; loans were advanced where needed for payment of visa fees and head taxes; special plans were evolved for . . . initial living expenses . . . with the understanding that local communities would take over if the need continued."

Nearly half chose to go to the New York City area. The war created severe housing shortages there, and for some, their first home was a refugee shelter opened in 1921 by HIAS. The agency provided comfortable living quarters, kosher kitchen facilities, and activities for the children. Many families stayed as long as six months until permanent housing was found, sometimes in five- or six-floor walkups in crowded tenement buildings. A few families, not deterred by the rigorous winter weather of the area, settled in nearby Syracuse and Rochester. Of the rest, 58 went to California, 55 to New Jersey, and the remaining 218 were scattered over

17 other states and the District of Columbia. The Coordinating Committee, which had spent nearly $250,000 on the refugees in a year and a half, disbanded.

The 23 babies born in Oswego were automatically American citizens. Of the original 982 refugees, 14 had died and 69 had already voluntarily departed to foreign countries of their choice. In July and August 1945,

Andre Waksman

Andre Waksman was just a baby when he arrived at Fort Ontario with his parents. The family, originally from Belgium, crossed over the Alps from France into Italy. With the closing of the shelter, Andre and his family received entry visas to the United States, and he became a naturalized citizen in 1951. Andre became an artist and filmmaker in France. His documentary film *1943, le temps d'un repit* (translated as "A Pause in the Holocaust") recalled the protection offered by the occupying Italian army in France to Jews—including his own family—before the Germans invaded.

two groups of residents sailed back to Yugoslavia. One group sent a letter to Malcolm Pitts, the shelter's acting director, expressing "our immense gratitude for the heart-felt hospitality we enjoyed during our whole residence at Fort Ontario. . . . We are leaving this country with the greatest admiration for the American people, with whom we would like to remain good friends."

The last resident left Fort Ontario on February 5, 1946, and the War Relocation Authority turned it back over to the US Army a few weeks later as the refugees began their new lives throughout the United States. While some continued to suffer from the effects of their experiences in Europe and were not successful, most adjusted well. The War Relocation Authority reported, "They have every promise of becoming loyal and productive Americans."

Paul Bokros said that their stay in Oswego "was responsible for the tremendous success we all achieved." They went on to varied professions: scientist, physician, filmmaker, engineer, photographer, artist, architect, lawyer, teacher, secretary, dentist, shop owner. Some benefited from the occupational classes sponsored by ORT back at the shelter. Women who took the beauty course found work as beauticians and hairdressers.

Often, the new citizens had to forget their previous occupations and accept other responsibilities. For some, it was necessary to adjust radically from their lives in Europe. Former furniture and department store owners in Europe became carpenters, upholsterers, and furniture repairers.

Egon Josefowitz, once a successful hat manufacturer and political leader in Germany, settled in Indianapolis, Indiana. Before coming to Fort Ontario, he had been imprisoned in several concentration camps and lost members of his immediate family. He became the beloved sexton of the United Hebrew Congregation. "For my old age," he told a reporter, "I am quite satisfied now. I like my work and I like the people here."

Nathan Weinstein, from Antwerp, Belgium, came to Oswego when he was nine years old. After release from the shelter, his family went to Brooklyn, New York. He became a rabbi, first teaching in New York and later in Dayton, Ohio.

Leon Levitch's musical education began while in a concentration camp in Italy. There, along with learning to play the piano, he had studied the basics of piano repair, which made him very popular in Oswego. Locals found out about his skill and hired him privately to tune their pianos. When the shelter closed, he made his way to California, where he studied music at UCLA and composed classical music. He supported himself by tuning pianos but achieved great acclaim for his musical compositions, which were performed and recorded.

Alfred Alalouf's family journey from Yugoslavia ended in Brooklyn, New York. Desperate to find a way out of Europe, they made their way through Albania and Italy. There, they boarded a ship heading to Spain that was sunk by a German mine. Clinging to the side of a lifeboat, the family was saved by a passing British ship and returned to shore, where they were selected to come to Fort Ontario. Alfred's first job after leaving the shelter was selling hot dogs on Coney Island. His son, Ben, who was born in a Yugoslavian bomb shelter in 1941, shined shoes as a child outside New

York subway stations. Ben went on to college and eventually became a high school history teacher and administrator.

Michael Kricer was 60 years old when he arrived in Oswego. He was born in Russia and served in the

Michael Kricer after leaving the shelter. Like other refugees, he began to rebuild his life.

Russian Army during World War I. He then moved to Yugoslavia, where he became a citizen and managed a textile factory.

With the outbreak of World War II, Michael tried to obtain visas for his family to emigrate to safety in another country. Before he could succeed, his wife Sophie and 10-year-old son Alexander were arrested in Yugoslavia and deported, never to be seen again. Now alone, Michael fled from place to place until he eventually reached Italy.

At the shelter, Michael actively participated in events and served as chief of the volunteer firemen. When the shelter closed, he moved to New York City and worked in textile sales. He then made a permanent home in Brookline, Massachusetts, where he met and married Minna Wies. In retirement, he took art lessons and enjoyed painting.

Joseph H. Smart, the shelter's first director who resigned to become a refugee advocate, was not forgotten. In May 1946, he was honored with the Franklin D. Roosevelt Award of the German Jewish newspaper *Aufbau*, as the "American who has done most for the welfare of new Americans and their integration."

Toward the very end of their confinement in Fort Ontario, artistic residents Miriam Sommerburg and Charles Abeles wrote and presented an operetta, *The*

Golden Cage, which summarized their 18 months in the shelter. The operetta began with a description of their arrival, when local Oswegonians stared at them from behind the barbed wire fence. In another scene, set over a year later, the refugees still felt a lack of freedom. Finally, there was joy when news reached the shelter that President Truman had allowed them to stay in the United States.

In 1981, the Syracuse Council of Pioneer Women, one of the local groups that came to the aid of the refugees, dedicated a historical monument at Fort Ontario to commemorate the 18 months. Survivor Adam Munz told those in attendance, "The Oswego Refugee Shelter was and has remained for me, and I suspect of some others as well, a paradox. It symbolized freedom from tyranny, oppression, and persecution on the one hand, and yet there was a fence, a gate that locked and guards were felt necessary to contain us at the very time we longed for the kind of freedom this country stood for and professed." A few years later the monument was defaced by vandals. The damage was never repaired, to remind visitors of the hurt that hatred causes.

Survivors have held several reunions since they left Fort Ontario. In 1984, they gathered in New York City to share experiences, some pleasant and some painful. "I was upset," Regina Gal remembered about her stay in the shelter, "but at least we got clothing, food, and shelter. At least we were clean." Abe Forman remembered the horror of being in concentration camps before arriving in Oswego. "You were blonde, you were killed," he said. "You were a louse, you were killed. You were strong, you were killed. They just killed. You can't believe the kind of hell it was."

At their fiftieth reunion in 1993, Manya Breuer, the first woman married at the shelter, recalled, "I feel this energy that was given to me to fully develop my life here in the United States and live in America as a human being . . . and being left from such a horror is to be like a messenger to let the world know what it is like to have faced a world of hate and prejudice and not letting any other human being live." At the 75th reunion, held in Oswego in 2019, 19 surviving refugees were present along with dozens of children and grandchildren of former shelter residents.

In 2002, one of the remaining structures at Fort Ontario, the old administration building, was converted into the Safe Haven Holocaust Refugee Shelter Museum to preserve the history of the place. That's where the stories of the 982 refugees now live on for future generations. Paul Lear, superintendent of the Fort Ontario State Historic Site, said, "Fort Ontario was the only refugee shelter in the United States during

The Golden Cage

———————

We are in a cage without reason,
We are in a cage, golden cage;
We're missing nothing but our freedom . . .

I feel myself a monkey
In the zoological garden;
Are we to be on display?
There's nothing missing but the warden!
What are we,—a sensation
For tedious people's pleasure? . . .

Behind the fence of Fort Ontario
We are sitting, awaiting the glorious day,
When our unchained feet may finally go
Over the most wonderful country's way.

There is no food we are longing for.
No material need we are suffering,
But our hearts have never been cared for,
Are ever tremendously troubled.

Like a lion in the cage
We are losing health and mood;
Like a bird, which after age
Finds its wings for nothing good. . . .

We send our thanks to Roosevelt
Who heard us beyond the stars,
Who sent an angel to the world
To free us from this farce. . . .

We soon leave Fort Ontario
And try to find our hearth;
To find our life, our work and move
At liberty on earth!

World War II, so it's historically unique. Oswego was a welcoming community. There were few serious problems, and local citizens formed a committee to address potential problems before the refugees arrived and assisted them until the end of the life of the shelter."

The story of the 982 refugees who arrived at Fort Ontario in 1944 is a small but important link in the larger history of the Holocaust. Many considered the creation of the shelter too little and too late for the millions who perished. Ruth Gruber later said, "We could have saved hundreds of thousands. . . . Our failure to do more is one of the blots on our history. It just breaks your heart." Yet, for those who arrived on the *Henry Gibbins* that August day, their lives and the lives of their children and grandchildren were changed forever.

With the passage of time, there will come a day when none of original Fort Ontario Shelter survivors remain. But as Dr. Rebecca Erbelding, curator and historian at the US Holocaust Memorial Museum, said, "It's our job to remember their story. . . . Fort Ontario then housed nearly 1,000 complete individuals with complex feelings and lives—with likes, dislikes, loves, losses, all the individual details that make people unique—and when we realize that, we get closer to understanding what an amazing and complicated place the shelter had been."

epilogue

The residents of the Emergency Refugee Shelter left Fort Ontario in 1946, but the city of Oswego remains forever linked with them. Mayor William J. Barlow Jr. said, "The story of the Fort Ontario refugees is a unique and significant piece of our local and national history. The City of Oswego opened its arms to the Fort Ontario refugees, and from that day forward, their story was woven into the fabric of our community." Speaking at a reunion of the refugees in 2019, the mayor said, "Oswego covets its role in history. We were the only place in the United States that was refuge to folks escaping the Holocaust."

Although the old barracks at Fort Ontario are long gone, the Safe Haven Holocaust Refugee Shelter

Museum draws visitors from around the world. It is a place of pride for the Oswego community, and every year local school children visit to learn of the role their city played in the lives of the refugees. According to Mayor Barlow, it is "what makes this community so special. It is a critical component to the transformation of Oswego."

The president of the museum, Kevin Hill, said, "To save one life is significant. To save 1,000 lives is more significant, but there is always the question of how many more lives could have been saved. This is the sentiment I hear expressed by the former refugees, but it is always predicated on an eternal gratefulness for being part of the group who were saved, an intense love of our country and expression of warmth for the people of Oswego, who welcomed the refugees with open arms."

Florence A. Farley remembered:

Having grown up in Oswego, New York, the Fort Ontario Holocaust Refugee Shelter was an important part of the pride of the community. It was made even more so because my mom, Florence Bronson Mahaney, actually worked at the shelter. You see, before the refugees arrived, local people were hired to prepare the facilities. She told us stories of making beds and setting up housing for these people. She was always a very good cook, so she helped out in the kitchen and learned much about kosher dietary laws that she found fascinating. She described having to break a plate because dairy had been placed on a plate reserved for meat. She was intrigued that some of the Orthodox families could eat tuna but not clams.

Finally, she kept photographs of the lovely wedding of refugees Manya and Ernst Breuer and learned about Jewish wedding traditions. She admired the work ethic of many of these recent arrivals to the US. When Ruth Gruber wrote her book *Haven* about the story of these refugees, my mom went to the bookstore in Syracuse to meet her but also to "correct" some of what she considered errors in the book. Even after being mildly chastised by this woman she had never met, Ruth was kind enough to sign her book, "To Florence Mahaney who walks among these pages." And since I, too, lived just steps from the sites within Fort Ontario where all of this took place, I was able to literally walk among the memories of not abstract refugees but the real people whose life stories my mom had shared.

acknowledgments

The idea for this book began with an email from my friend Florence Farley of Oswego, New York. Knowing of my interest in history, she invited me to Oswego for the 75th anniversary commemoration of the Fort Ontario Emergency Refugee Shelter. I knew a bit about the shelter and had referred to it in Holocaust courses I'd taught. But not until I was in Oswego and heard firsthand accounts of surviving residents did this book start taking shape. It's a story that needed to be told.

For their assistance, I am grateful to Paul Lear, superintendent of the Fort Ontario State Historic Site; Kevin Hill, president of the Safe Haven Holocaust Refugee Shelter Museum; William Barlow Jr., mayor of Oswego; Kathryn Johns-Masten, librarian, Penfield

Library, SUNY Oswego; and Jonathan Burg. A special thank-you to Dr. Rebecca Erbelding, curator and historian, US Holocaust Memorial Museum, for her valuable advice and insight.

I am most appreciative of my editor Jerome Pohlen and the wonderful folks at Chicago Review Press for their caring expertise. To my wife, Rosalind, my first editor, a loving thank-you for her continued patience and understanding.

citizenship of fort ontario refugees

NATIONALITY	TOTAL REFUGEES	NUMBER OF JEWS
Austrian	235	210
Belgian	3	0
Bulgarian	4	4
Czechoslovakian	41	34
Danziger	8	7
Dutch	1	1
French	15	15
German	96	85
Greek	4	0
Hungarian	3	3

NATIONALITY	TOTAL REFUGEES	NUMBER OF JEWS
Italian	2	1
Libyan	4	4
Polish	146	140
Rumania	17	17
Russian	17	9
Spanish	5	5
Turkish	10	10
Yugoslavian	369	326
Stateless	2	0
Total	**982**	**874**

time line

///////////////////////////////////

1924 The Immigration Act of 1924 limits yearly immigration visas to 2 percent of the total number of people of each nationality in the United States as of the 1890 national census.

1933 The Nazi Party, led by Adolf Hitler, comes to power in Germany.

1938 Kristallnacht. On the night of November 9–10, planned violence is unleashed against Jews throughout Nazi Germany. Synagogues and Jewish businesses are burned. Thousands of people are sent to concentration camps.

1939 World War II begins with the German invasion of Poland.

1940 German armies expand into France, Belgium, and Holland.

The Auschwitz concentration camp opens.

1941 Jews in Nazi Germany are forced to wear a yellow star.

Yugoslavia is invaded by German troops.

The United States enters World War II.

1942 At the Wannsee Conference in Berlin, the Nazis make plans for their "Final Solution" against Europe's Jews.

Riegner telegram reveals the Nazis' ongoing mass murders of Jews.

1943 Uprising in Warsaw ghetto.

Allied forces land in Southern Italy.

1944 President Roosevelt creates the War Refugee Board.

US Fifth Army liberates Rome, June 1944.

Allied troops invade Normandy.

Refugees arrive at Fort Ontario, August 5.

Eleanor Roosevelt visits the Fort Ontario Shelter, September 20.

1945 Nine shelter students enroll in the Oswego State Teachers College.

President Roosevelt dies, April 12.

Germany surrenders, May 8.

Director Joseph Smart resigns to dedicate his time to helping the refugees stay in the United States.

Japan surrenders, August 14.

President Harry Truman issues an order permitting shelter residents to stay in the United States.

1946 Shelter residents make the trip to Canada and return with valid visas to live in the United States. They scatter to create new lives.

notes

1: The Arrival

"I cannot tell you": "At America's First 'Free Port,'" *Wisconsin Jewish Chronicle* (Milwaukee, WI), September 15, 1944.

"looked haggard": US War Relocation Authority and Edward B. Marks, *Token Shipment: The Story of American's War Refugee Shelter* (Washington, DC: US Government Printing Office, 1946), 19.

"Some of the families": "Mrs. Zuckman Has List of Oswego Shelter Refugees," *Daily Record* (Long Branch, NJ), August 16, 1944.

"We had all this food": Claudia Rice, "59 Years Ago, They Fled to an Internment Camp," *New York Times*, July 21, 2003.

"It was fascinating": Oswego County Oral History Program, tape OH279 transcript, Penfield Library, SUNY Oswego, 2.

"It is hard to imagine": Oswego County Oral History Program, tape OH279 transcript, 4.

"My first breakfast": Oswego County Oral History Program, tape OH270 transcript, Penfield Library, SUNY Oswego, 20.

2: Marked by War

"They lived": United States War Relocation Authority and Marks, *Token Shipment*, 10.

"It has become necessary": "The Immigration Act of 1924," History, Art & Archives of the US House of Representatives, accessed November 2, 2020, https://history .house.gov/Historical-Highlights/1901-1950/The -Immigration-Act-of-1924/.

"I wrote, telephoned": US House Committee on Immigration and Naturalization, *Investigation of Problems Presented by Refugees at Fort Ontario Refugee Shelter*, 79th Cong., 1st Sess., June 25 & 26, 1945 (Washington, DC: US Government Printing Office, 1945), 156. "Dickstein hearings" on future reference.

"to put every obstacle": "Breckinridge Long Memorandum Text," Facing History and Ourselves, accessed November 2, 2020, https://facinghistory.org/resource-library/text /breckinridge-long-memorandum-text.

"Charity ought to begin": *Appendix to the Congressional Record*, June 7, 1939, 2424–2425.

"In the desperate": US War Relocation Authority and Marks, *Token Shipment*, 10.

"These thousand people came": Dickstein hearings, 148.

"We left everything behind": Dickstein hearings, 155.

"I had city clothes": Oswego County Oral History Program, tape OH270 transcript, 18.

"The Italians": "Joseph Goebbels Complains of Italians' treatment of Jews," History.com, updated December 11, 2019, www.history.com/this-day-in-history/goebbels -complains-of-italians-treatment-of-jews.

"In Rome": Dickstein hearings, 167.

"I must say": Oswego County Oral History Program, tape OH275 transcript, Penfield Library, SUNY Oswego, 2.

"We appeal to you" and *"We shall do"*: Norman H. Finkelstein, *JPS Guide to American Jewish History* (Philadelphia: Jewish Publication Society, 2007), 139.

"temporary protection": Rafael Medoff, "Why Did Gallup Omit Its Own Holocaust Poll?" *Washington (DC) Examiner,* December 10, 2018, https://www.washingtonexaminer .com/weekly-standard/why-did-gallup-omit-its-own -holocaust-poll.

"to take action": "Roosevelt Sets Up War Refugee Board," *New York Times,* January 23, 1944.

"From now on": "Records of the War Refugee Board, 1944–1945," box 25, folder 15, Franklin D. Roosevelt Presidential Library and Museum.

"I feel it is important": Karen Greenberg, ed., *Columbia University Library, New York: The Varian Fry Papers; The Fort Ontario Emergency Refugee Shelter Papers* (New York: Garland Publishing, 1990), 141.

"will be brought": US War Relocation Authority and Marks, *Token Shipment,* 4.

"Care should be used": Greenberg, ed., *Columbia,* 4.

"families and survivors": "Safe Haven Museum and Education Center," Gluseum, accessed November 2, 2020, https:// www.gluseum.com/US/Oswego/133896493348606 /Safe-Haven-Museum-and-Education-Center.

"He is an Austrian": "Records of the War Refugee Board, 1944–1945," box 29, folder 7, Franklin D. Roosevelt Presidential Library and Museum.

3: Journey to a New Life

"To share the burden": Dickstein hearings, 99.

"include a reasonable": US War Relocation Authority and Marks, *Token Shipment,* 9.

"The refugees will": Greenberg, ed., *Columbia,* 145.

"would never be": US War Relocation Authority and Marks, *Token Shipment*, 22.

"It's only a form": Joseph H. Smart, *Don't Fence Me In: Fort Ontario Refugees; How They Won Their Freedom* (Salt Lake City: Heritage Arts, 1991), 41.

"He was reported": Smart, 41.

"Departure for": Dickstein hearings, 179.

"We had nothing": Oswego County Oral History Program, tape OH275 transcript, 3.

"I found myself": Safe Haven Museum and Education Center, *Don't Fence Me In! Memories of the Fort Ontario Refugees and Their Friends* (Oswego, NY: Safe Haven Museum and Education Center, 2013), 21.

"A few days later": Oswego County Oral History Program, tape OH275 transcript, 20.

"Mr. Secretary" and *"You're right"*: Oswego County Oral History Program, tape OH270 transcript, 2.

"It was very cramped": "Safe Haven Museum," Gluseum, https://www.gluseum.com/US/Oswego/133896493348606/Safe-Haven-Museum-and-Education-Center.

"Quarters and latrines": Greenberg, ed., *Columbia*, 158.

"the refugees know": Greenberg, ed., 152.

"I never saw": Safe Haven Museum, *Don't Fence Me In!*, 45.

"it leaves a trail": Greenberg, ed., *Columbia*, 159.

"If you're coming": "Safe Haven Museum," Gluseum, https://www.gluseum.com/US/Oswego/133896493348606/Safe-Haven-Museum-and-Education-Center.

"The whitewashed barracks": Safe Haven Museum, *Don't Fence Me In!*, 35.

"On behalf": "Oswego Welcomes Refugees at Fort Ontario," *JTA Daily Bulletin* (New York, NY), August 7, 1944.

"Whenever there is a knock": Lawrence Baron, "Haven from the Holocaust," *New York History*, January 1983, 10.

"was the first time": "Refugees Sheltered at Fort Ontario," *Pulaski (NY) Democrat*, August 10, 1944.

4: Life Behind the Fence

"We are in a cage": Safe Haven Museum, *Don't Fence Me In!*, 115.

"He's never seen": Elizabeth Wilson, "Refugees in U.S. Camp Show Results of Hitler's Horrors," *Gazette and Daily* (York, PA), August 10, 1944.

"Only the absolute": Eleanor Roosevelt, "Refugees Decorate Camp, Make Own Fun," *Akron (OH) Journal*, September 22, 1944.

"A typical menu": Todd Wright, "Refugees Find Safety at Oswego," *New York Daily News*, August 21, 1944, 26.

"after hiding" and *"don't laugh"*: Adelaide Kerr, "European Youth Ills Are Peril," *Arizona Republic* (Phoenix, AZ), June 3, 1945.

"Papa, because I hear": "Son Finds Parents in Refugee Camp," *New York Times*, August 10, 1944, 5.

"opened my big mouth": Jeffrey Schmalz, "At Albany Exhibit, Memories of a Wartime Refugee Camp," *New York Times*, January 28, 1986, section B, 1.

"crawling through": Safe Haven Museum, *Don't Fence Me In!*, 34.

"And we went": Oswego County Oral History Program, tape OH279 transcript, 4.

"Eat it" and *"In Europe"*: Cross, "At America's First 'Free Port.'"

"Prior to the coming": Safe Haven Museum, *Don't Fence Me In!*, 31.

"The concert was fine": Oswego County Oral History Program, tape OH279 transcript, 14.

"Restrictions are plentiful": Eleanor Roosevelt, My Day, *Long Beach (CA) Independent*, September 25, 1944.

"impossible to maintain" and *"to leave the barracks"*: US War Relocation Authority and Marks, *Token Shipment*, 41.

"Four residents suffered": Smart, *Don't Fence Me In*, 32.

"The garbage is an interesting": US War Relocation Authority and Marks, *Token Shipment*, 41.

"to keep the figure": Greenberg, ed., *Columbia*, 215.

"Listening to the lectures": John B. Clark, W Bruce Leslie, et al., *SUNY at Sixty: The Promise of the State University of New York* (Albany, NY: SUNY Press, 2010), 48.

"they possessed everything": US War Relocation Authority, *WRA: A Story of Human Conservation* (Washington, DC: US Government Printing Office, 1946), 167.

"I felt deceived": "Safe Haven Museum," Gluseum, accessed November 2, 2020, https://www.gluseum.com/US/Oswego/133896493348606/Safe-Haven-Museum-and-Education-Center.

"be neighborly": "Church Organizes Plan for Fellowship with European Refugees," *Advance-News* (Ogdensburg, NY), January 28, 1945, 10.

"It is my opinion": Greenberg, ed., *Columbia*, 198.

"we are fed": "Christmas," *Ontario Chronicle* (Oswego, NY), December 21, 1944, 3.

"Whether our guiding light": "Christmas Greetings to the Residents of Fort Ontario," *Ontario Chronicle* (Oswego, NY), December 21, 1944, 3.

5: Like Other Children

"Foreigners are real people.": Naomi Jolles, "The Fourth R," *Woman's Home Companion*, July 1945, 16.

"I was a man": Oswego County Oral History Program, tape OH275 transcript, 10.

"as they looked": Oswego County Oral History Program, tape OH278 transcript, Penfield Library, SUNY Oswego, 1.

"The teachers": Philip Slomovitz, Purely Commentary, *Detroit Jewish News*, August 12, 1983.

"We shall be very happy": Clark, Leslie, et al., *SUNY at Sixty*, 47.

"to be happy": Oswego County Oral History Program, tape OH275 transcript, 10.

"In prison camp": Dickstein hearings, 148.

"Your children are now" through *"We are happy"*: Greenberg, ed., *Columbia*, 207.

"At first a lot": Jolles, "The Fourth R," 16.

"They did inspire": Jolles, 16.

"first normal teenage life": "Oral History Interview with Edith Klein and Lillian Glass," US Holocaust Memorial Museum, 1984 (RG-50-413-0006).

"They were people" and *"Oh, then"*: Dickstein hearings, 147.

"How quickly": Oswego County Oral History Program, tape OH278 transcript, 3.

"The fresh and rather cold": Dickstein hearings, 173.

"fitted in very nicely": Oswego County Oral History Program, tape OH278 transcript, 53.

"They built their fire": Oswego County Oral History Program, tape OH278 transcript, 8.

"I can't get over": "Scouting in a World War II Refugee Troop," *Scouting*, October 2004.

"It was a good happy time": Oswego County Oral History Program, tape OH275 transcript, 7.

"Leaving this country": Clark, Leslie, et al., *SUNY at Sixty*, 47.

6: To Stay or Not to Stay

"At the end of the war": Safe Haven Museum, *Don't Fence Me In!*, 16.

"There was a fence": US War Relocation Authority, *WRA: A Story of Human Conservation*, 168.

"will be returned": Greenberg, ed., *Columbia*, 145.

"They fretted": Charles J. Wellner, "No Place for Jews in Post-war Europe," *Abilene (TX) Reporter-News*, April 6, 1945, 5.

"They seem gay" and *"I will never go back"*: "Despair Grips Refugees Here," *Arizona Republic* (Phoeniz, AZ), April 8, 1945.

"Be our lawyer": Dr. Ernst Wolff, letter to First Lady Eleanor Roosevelt, February 1, 1945, record group 48, "Central Classified Files, 1907–1972," Records of the Office of the Secretary of the Interior, National Archives at College Park.

"We, residents of this shelter": "Gratitude to the United States," *Ontario Chronicle* (Oswego, NY), June 14, 1945, 2.

"taken on the psychological": "Release of Anti-Nazi Refugees Urged," *Poughkeepsie (NY) Journal*, July 16, 1945.

"to live and work" and *"While Americans are"*: "More Flexibility Please," *Ontario Chronicle* (Oswego, NY), June 14, 1945, 3.

"Why should the residents": Smart, *Don't Fence Me In*, 56.

"so that I will": Smart, 77.

"My sole objective": "Mr. Smart Has Resigned," *Ontario Chronicle* (Oswego, NY), May 10, 1945, 1.

"It is important": Smart, *Don't Fence Me In*, 72.

"I propose to enlist": Smart, 2.

"received enthusiastic" and *"has always shown"*: Smart, 76.

"The speech of Mr. Smart": Edmund Landau, "A Good Fighter for Freedom," *Ontario Chronicle* (Oswego, NY), May 10, 1945, 3.

"So, I am alone": Dickstein hearings, 164.

"Here is an opportunity": Joseph Smart, letter to Eleanor Roosevelt, series 1, 1945, Franklin D. Roosevelt Presidential Library and Museum.

"These refugees came": "Wants Refugees Returned," *New York Daily News*, July 18, 1945, 12.

"It is the American way": Greenberg, ed., *Columbia*, 206.

"Driven from their homes": Dickstein hearings, 16.

"Surely it seems": Records of the War Refugee Board, 1944–1945, box 29, folder 8, Franklin D. Roosevelt Presidential Library and Museum.

"I'm very satisfied here": Dickstein hearings, 165.

"besieged by pressure groups": "Urges Permanent Visit by Refugees," *Morning News* (Wilmington, DE), May 16, 1945.

"they be permitted": Dickstein hearings, 8.

"I think you would make": Dickstein hearings, 30.

"The people are completely": Dickstein hearings, 50.

"There would be no": Dickstein hearings, 54.

"You think" and *"I think"*: Dickstein hearings, 61.

"These boys": US War Relocation Authority and Marks, *Token Shipment*, 57.

"No, sir": Dickstein hearings, 76.

"They are a very talented": Dickstein hearings, 97.

"We have been here": Dickstein hearings, 92.

"I was to call": *Congressional Record*, 79th Congress, vol. 91, part 12, August 6, 1945, A4233.

"The present confinement": *Congressional Record*, A4234.

"It is up to Congress": Greenberg, ed., *Columbia*, 255.

"In the name": Greenberg, ed., *Columbia*, 255.

"If we don't give": "To President Truman," *Ontario Chronicle* (Oswego, NY), August 9, 1945, 3.

"We would like to present" and *"This letter"*: Greenberg, ed., *Columbia*, 257–258.

7: When the Gates Opened

"Now all is behind me": US War Relocation Authority and Marks, *Token Shipment*, 87.

"give the guest": "Statement of the Friends of Fort Ontario Guest-Refugees," Eleanor Roosevelt Papers, series 1, 1945, Franklin D. Roosevelt Presidential Library and Museum.

"This is the opportunity": Harry Schneiderman and Julius Maller, eds., "Immigration and Refugee Aid," *The American Jewish Year Book*, vol. 48, *1946–1947* (Philadelphia: Jewish Publication Society, 1946), 219.

"In the circumstances": "Statement and Directive by the President on Immigration to the United States of Certain Displaced Persons and Refugees in Europe," December 22, 1945, Harry S. Truman Library and Museum, https://www.trumanlibrary.gov/library/public-papers/225/statement-and-directive-president-immigration-united-states-certain.

"But it was activity": Oswego County Oral History Program, tape OH279 transcript, 9.

"All in all": US War Relocation Authority and Marks, *Token Shipment*, 76.

"It's wonderful": "92 Refugees Cross Border as Legal U.S. Residents," *Democrat and Chronicle* (Rochester, NY), January 18, 1946.

"Arrangements were made": Schneiderman and Maller, eds., "Immigration and Refugee Aid," *American Jewish Year Book*, 222.

"our immense gratitude": Letter to Malcolm Pitts, record group 48, "Central Classified Files, 1907–1972," Records of the Office of the Secretary of the Interior, National Archives at College Park.

"They have every promise": James C. Munn, "War Refugees Find Homes in America," *Ithaca (NY) Journal*, February 13, 1947.

"was responsible for": Clark, Leslie, et al., *SUNY at Sixty*, 49

"For my old age": Virginia Childers, "Refugee Finds Haven Here," *Indianapolis Star*, March 9, 1947.

"American who has done": "Immigrants Honor Earl Harrison, Joseph Smart," *Wisconsin Jewish Chronicle* (Milwaukee, WI), May 17, 1946.

"The Oswego Refugee Shelter": Oswego County Oral History
Program, tape OH279 transcript, 9.

"I was upset" and *"You were blonde"*: "Reunited, Survivors
Recall the Holocaust," *Philadelphia Inquirer*, August 4, 1984.

"I feel this energy": Safe Haven Museum, *Don't Fence Me In!*, 21.

"Fort Ontario was": Paul Lear, digital correspondence with
author, January 6, 2020.

"The Golden Cage": US War Relocation Authority and Marks,
Token Shipment, 84–85.

"We could have saved": "Holocaust Refugees Recall Their New
York Imprisonment," *Bennington (VT) Banner*, March 10,
1986, 14.

"It is our job": Dr. Rebecca Erbelding, digital correspondence
with author, January 7, 2020.

Epilogue

"The story": William Barlow, letter to author, August 5, 2019.

"Oswego covets" and *"what makes"*: William Barlow, speech to
reunion of Fort Ontario Shelter refugees, August 5, 2019.

"To save one life": Kevin Hill, digital correspondence with
author, September 17, 2020.

"Having grown up": Florence A. Farley, digital correspondence
with author, September 23, 2020.

bibliography

BOOKS

Clark, John B., W. Bruce Leslie, et al. *SUNY at Sixty: The Promise of the State University of New York*. Albany, NY: SUNY Press, 2010.

Erbelding, Rebecca. *Rescue Board: The Untold Story of America's Efforts to Save the Jews of Europe*. New York: Doubleday, 2018.

Finkelstein, Norman H. *JPS Guide to American Jewish History*. Philadelphia: Jewish Publication Society, 2007.

Finkelstein, Norman H. *Remember Not to Forget: A Memory of the Holocaust*. New York: Franklin Watts, 1987.

Greenberg, Karen, ed. *Columbia University Library, New York: The Varian Fry Papers; The Fort Ontario Emergency Refugee Shelter Papers*. New York: Garland Publishing, 1990.

Gruber, Ruth. *Haven: The Unknown Story of 1,000 World War II Refugees*. New York: Coward-McCann, 1983.

Lowenstein, Sharon. *Token Refuge: The Story of the Jewish Refugee Shelter at Oswego, 1944–1946*. Bloomington, IN: Indiana University Press, 1986.

171

Safe Haven Museum and Education Center. *Don't Fence Me In! Memories of the Fort Ontario Refugees and Their Friends*. Oswego, NY: Safe Haven Museum and Education Center, 2013.

Schneiderman, Harry, and Julius Maller, eds. *The American Jewish Year Book*, vol. 48, 1946–1947. Philadelphia: Jewish Publication Society, 1946.

Smart, Joseph H. *Don't Fence Me In: Fort Ontario Refugees; How They Won Their Freedom*. Salt Lake City: Heritage Arts, 1991.

US House Committee on Immigration and Naturalization. *Investigation of Problems Presented by Refugees at Fort Ontario Refugee Shelter*, 79th Cong., 1st Sess., June 25 & 26, 1945.

US War Refugee Board. *Final Summary Report of the Executive Director, War Refugee Board*. Washington, DC, 1945.

US War Relocation Authority. *WRA: A Story of Human Conservation*. Washington, DC: US Government Printing Office, 1946.

US War Relocation Authority and Edward B. Marks. *Token Shipment: The Story of American's War Refugee Shelter*. Washington, DC: US Government Printing Office, 1946.

Warnes, Kathy, Liz Kahl, and Kevin Hill. *Don't Fence Me In: Memories of the Fort Ontario Refugees and Their Friends*. Oswego, NY: Safe Haven Museum and Education Center, 2013.

Wyman, David S. *The Abandonment of the Jews: America and the Holocaust 1941–1945*. New York: New Press, 1984.

NEWSPAPERS

Abilene (TX) Reporter-News
Advance-News (Ogdensburg, NY)
Akron (OH) Journal
Arizona Republic (Phoenix, AZ)
Bennington (VT) Banner

Daily Record (Long Branch, NJ)
Democrat and Chronicle (Rochester, NY)
Detroit Jewish News
Gazette and Daily (York, PA)
Indianapolis Star
Ithaca (NY) Journal
JTA Daily Bulletin (New York, NY)
Long Beach (CA) Independent
Morning News (Wilmington, DE)
New York Daily News
New York Times
Ontario Chronicle (Oswego, NY)
Philadelphia Inquirer
Poughkeepsie (NY) Journal
Pulaski (NY) Democrat
Washington (DC) Examiner
Wisconsin Jewish Chronicle (Milwaukee, WI)

OTHER

New York History
Scouting
Woman's Home Companion

WEBSITES

Franklin D. Roosevelt Presidential Library and Museum, http://www.fdrlibrary.org

Gluseum, http://www.gluseum.com

Oswego County Oral History Program, Penfield Library, SUNY Oswego, http://www.oswego.edu/library/oral-histories-emergency-refugee-shelter-fort-ontario-safe-haven

Safe Haven Holocaust Refugee Shelter Museum, http://www.safehavenmuseum.com

US Holocaust Memorial Museum, http://www.ushmm.org

image credits

Page 2: US Naval and Heritage Command (NH 96577)

Page 3: United States Holocaust Memorial Museum, courtesy of National Archives and Records Administration, College Park, Maryland (18399)

Page 5: National Archives and Records Administration (210.3-CFZ-1-230)

Page 7: United States Holocaust Memorial Museum, courtesy of National Archives and Records Administration, College Park, Maryland (18399)

Page 8: National Archives and Records Administration (210.3-CFZ-1-230)

Page 10: United States Holocaust Memorial Museum, courtesy of National Archives and Records Administration, College Park, Maryland (18396)

Page 11: United States Holocaust Memorial Museum, courtesy of National Archives and Records Administration, College Park, Maryland (60000)

Page 14: United States Holocaust Memorial Museum, courtesy of Michel Reynders (65974)

Page 15: United States Holocaust Memorial Museum, courtesy of Michael Blain (99604)

Page 16: United States Holocaust Memorial Museum, courtesy of National Archives and Records Administration (Duker Dwork-OSS-731918)

Page 17: National Archives and Records Administration (540179)

Page 21: Library of Congress (LC-USZ62-117148)

Page 23: National Archives and Records Administration (559369)

Page 24: National Archives and Records Administration (540124), courtesy of Archives of Macedonia (93126)

Page 26: United States Holocaust Memorial Museum (44665)

Page 27, top: United States Holocaust Memorial Museum, courtesy of Instytot Pamieci Narodowej (00001)

Page 27, bottom: United States Holocaust Memorial Museum, courtesy of Yad Vashem (77258)

Page 29: United States Holocaust Memorial Museum, courtesy of Simon Krauthamer (0047)

Page 30: United States Holocaust Memorial Museum, courtesy of Charles Martin Roman (37966)

Page 31: United States Holocaust Memorial Museum, courtesy of National Archives and Records Administration (60013)

Page 32: Library of Congress (LC-A6196-05744)

Page 34: United States Holocaust Memorial Museum (37968)

Page 36: United States Holocaust Memorial Museum, courtesy of Miriam Gery (60495)

Page 37: United States Holocaust Memorial Museum, courtesy of Walter Greenberg (49322)

Page 38: United States Holocaust Memorial Museum, courtesy of Instytut Pamieci Narodowej (15872)

Page 42: United States Holocaust Memorial Museum, courtesy of Franklin D. Roosevelt Library (85936)

Page 45: Library of Congress (LC-USW3-032-495 E)

Page 51: National Archives and Records Administration (RG 210 CFZ-106)

Page 55: United States Holocaust Memorial Museum, courtesy of Marion Michel Oliner (97473)

Page 59: United States Holocaust Memorial Museum, courtesy of National Archives and Records Administration (60021)

Page 61: Library of Congress (LC-DIG-ppprs-00368)

Page 63: National Archives and Records Administration (210.3-CFZ-1-230)

Page 64: National Archives and Records Administration (210.3-CFZ-1-230)

Page 68: United States Holocaust Memorial Museum, courtesy of Naomi Deutscher (85373)

Page 70, top: Library of Congress (LC-USE6-D-009275)

Page 70, bottom left: Library of Congress (LC-USE6-D-008764)

Page 70, bottom right: Library of Congress (LC-USE6-D-0045105)

Page 72: Library of Congress (LC-USW3-031507)

Page 74: United States Holocaust Memorial Museum (60020), courtesy of National Archives and Records Administration (210.3-CFZ-1-230)

Page 76: United States Holocaust Memorial Museum, courtesy of National Archives and Records Administration, College Park, Maryland (09602)

Page 77: National Archives and Records Administration (RG210 CFZ 201)

Page 81: National Archives and Records Administration (RG210 CFZ-226)

Page 84: Franklin D. Roosevelt Presidential Library (51-88-244 (6))

Page 85: United States Holocaust Memorial Museum, courtesy of Simon Krauthamer (05054)

Page 87: United States Holocaust Memorial Museum, courtesy of Tamar Hendel-Fishman (43812)

Page 88: United States Holocaust Memorial Museum, courtesy of Hans Thalheimer (06497)

Page 91: United States Holocaust Memorial Museum, courtesy of David Hendell (38542)

Page 94: United States Holocaust Memorial Museum, courtesy of Dr. Hans Thalheimer (06496)

Page 97, top: Oswego Public Library (IC-003)

Page 97, bottom: Oswego Public Library

Page 98: United States Holocaust Memorial Museum, courtesy of H. Brecher (85391)

Page 102: United States Holocaust Memorial Museum, courtesy of David Hendell (38545)

Page 105: United States Holocaust Memorial Museum, courtesy of David Hendell (38546)

Page 106: United States Holocaust Memorial Museum, courtesy of Walter Greenberg (49327)

Page 107: United States Holocaust Memorial Museum

Page 111: Library of Congress

Page 112: Oswego Public Library (IC-008)

Page 114: United States Holocaust Memorial Museum, courtesy of National Archives and Records Administration (60044)

Page 117: National Archives and Records Administration (RG210 CFZ-116)

Page 121: United States Holocaust Memorial Museum, courtesy of David Hendell (38547)

Page 129: United States Holocaust Memorial Museum (1989.316.5)

Page 136: United States Holocaust Memorial Museum, courtesy of National Archives and Records Administration (60038)

Page 142: Jonathan Burg

index

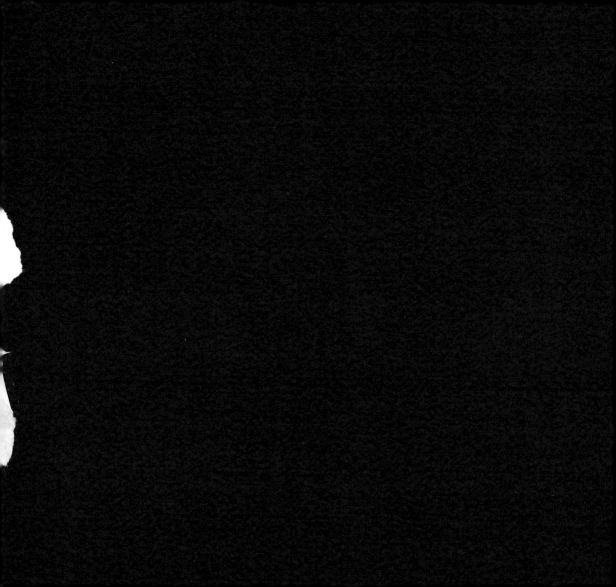